SOCCER

About the Author

In 1991, the University of San Francisco soccer team celebrated the 450th win of their coach, Steve Negoesco, the winningest coach in US collegiate soccer history. His accomplishments are many. Steve captained the USF soccer team to the first collegiate co-championship in St. Louis against Penn State on January 1, 1950. This event was later dubbed the first Soccer Super Bowl between the winners of the East and the West.

Steve was twice All-American, first on the west coast and as an alternate to the 1950 US National team. He began coaching while a student at USF in 1949 and continued after graduation to form the San Francisco Junior Soccer League in 1953. He is presently a member of the USF and Northern California Hall of Fame.

After receiving a Master's degree in biology, he taught for 30 years in the San Francisco Unified School District and coached as many as 11 youth teams a year. In 1961, Steve started coaching college soccer at his alma mater. In 1966, he gave up his other jobs as Secretary of the San Francisco Junior Soccer League and as a coach of youth soccer. He won a total of 8 national championships—as a player (1950), as a junior coach for Hakoah A.C. (1961), at USF (1966, 1975–76, 1978, and 1980)—and the Dewar Cup in 1975 with the San Francisco Italian Athletic Club.

At the collegiate level, his teams initiated the present East-West games among colleges and universities playing as many as 7 games in 12 days on the road.

From 1978–86 he involved himself again in youth coaching in northern California, held a multitude of coaching sessions for parents, and was a guest speaker for physical education coaches. He has coached over 3,000 games in his career.

He is a strong proponent of the zone style of soccer and the development of creativity and positive tactics in the game. As he sees it, "This is what future soccer will be like."

SOCCER

Stephen Negoesco
University of San Francisco

WCB
McGraw-Hill

Boston, Massachusetts   Burr Ridge, Illinios   Dubuque, Iowa
Madison, Wisconsin   New York, New York   San Francisco, California   St. Louis, Missouri

WCB/McGraw-Hill

A Division of The McGraw-Hill Companies

Book Team

Editor *Chris Rogers*
Developmental Editor *Susan J. McCormick*
Production Coordinator *Karen L. Nickolas*

Vice President and General Manager *Thomas E. Doran*
Executive Managing Editor *Ed Bartell*
Executive Editor *Edgar J. Laube*
Director of Marketing *Kathy Law Laube*
National Sales Manager *Eric Ziegler*
Marketing Manager *Pamela S. Cooper*
Advertising Manager *Jodi Rymer*
Managing Editor, Production *Colleen A. Yonda*
Manager of Visuals and Design *Faye M. Schilling*

Production Editorial Manager *Vickie Caughron*
Publishing Services Manager *Karen J. Slaght*
Permissions/Records Manager *Connie Allendorf*

Chairman Emeritus *Wm. C. Brown*
Chairman and Chief Executive Officer *Mark C. Falb*
President and Chief Operating Officer *G. Franklin Lewis*
Corporate Vice President, Operations *Beverly Kolz*
Corporate Vice President, President of WCB Manufacturing *Roger Meyer*

Cover photo by *Bob Coyle*

Cover design by *Jeanne M. Regan*

Copy editor *Rosemary Wallner*

Consulting Editor
Physical Education
Aileene Lockhart
Texas Women's University

Sports and Fitness Series
Evaluation Materials Editor
Jane A. Mott
Texas Women's University

Copyright © 1993 by Wm. C. Brown Communications, Inc. All rights reserved

Library of Congress Catalog Card Number: 91–74023

ISBN 0–697–10059–6   *TOC*

Printed in the United States of America

10 9 8 7 6 5 4 3 2

To all the soccer players in my family:
my children, Stephen, Sandra, Sonia,
Stuart, Sylvana, and Sergio, and
the referee, my wife, Mercedes.

Contents

Preface

Historically soccer has commanded very little positive notoriety in the U.S. Over 15,000,000 young people (boys and girls) are playing.

The game keeps changing and coaching methods must keep up, focusing on present demands. The total life activity level of prospects must be considered when preparing practice sessions and long-term season planning.

This book explains multiple ways of reaching this goal. All you are reading in this text is based on over 40 years of coaching and is not a copy of someone else's experiences. Some historical facts on game attendance and early beginnings have been obtained courtesy of the Soccer Historian Sam Foulds.

Soccer in America

1

Soccer came to America in the mid-1800s with immigrants from western Europe's large industrialized areas. Several eastern U.S. colleges began competing against each other. Princeton, Columbia, Rutgers, and Yale eventually adopted uniform rules, including one that fixed the number of players on a team at 11.

In 1894, the American League of Professional Football was established along the eastern seaboard. The entrepreneurs in charge were owners of the baseball teams in Baltimore, Boston, Brooklyn, Philadelphia, New York, and Washington. Most of those hired to run the clubs were baseball managers. The league collapsed, however, when some clubs imported professional players, compelling a few owners to cease operation. The only league left was an amateur one, the American Football Association, which started in 1884 and lasted until 1899.

In 1906 professional soccer reorganized, but the league was not interested in expanding the game nationally and thus fell from the professional ranks.

Another organization, the United States of America Football Association, a New York-based group, requested affiliation with the Federation of International Football Associations (FIFA), and provisional membership was granted in 1913. The new organization was affiliated with other associations in different areas of the U.S.; these areas, in turn, were in charge of various leagues that were made up of native talent and immigrant players. The game flourished at the amateur level, but it maintained its strong ethnic background and was therefore isolated from the mainstream of American sports.

Strong teams of semiprofessional players helped develop many youth teams. The promotion of youth soccer by the United States Youth Soccer Association (USYSA), and later by the American Youth Soccer Organization (AYSO), and the publicity surrounding the newly formed professional leagues brought the game to a new level of popularity among American youth in the late 1960s.

The USYSA is made up of state associations. The states are divided into districts, and the districts into leagues of boys and girls at various levels, from ages 4 to 19. The association initiates and promotes uniform rules, games, and tournaments at state, regional, national, and international levels.

FIFA is in charge of soccer throughout the world; it has 160 member countries. It promotes various international competitions, including the World Cup, which is played every four years. Independent of FIFA and the United States Soccer Federation (USSF, formerly the United States of America Football Association) is the NCAA (National Collegiate Athletic Association), with over 1,200 teams in divisions I, II, and III (colleges and universities), as well as junior colleges and NAIA (National Association of Intercollegiate Athletics) schools.

Separate from the NCAA is the huge pool of high school teams, where many young players develop through the parent-led, grass-roots movement of youth soccer.

U.S. soccer history is discussed in greater detail in "A History of the Game," in *America's Soccer Heritage* by Sam Foulds and Paul Harris, published in 1979 by Soccer for Americans, Box 836, Manhattan Beach, CA 90266. This book includes interesting facts about the game. Did you know, for instance, that . . .

- Soccer is America's original "football."
- In 1620, when the Pilgrims arrived at Plymouth, American Indians often played a game similar to soccer on the beaches of Greater Boston.
- Boston high school boys played soccer on Boston Common in 1862.
- The first intercollegiate "football" game in the United States, played between Princeton and Rutgers at New Brunswick, New Jersey, in 1869, was soccer.
- The Bristol County (Massachusetts) Soccer League, the first in America, was organized at Fall River, Massachusetts, in 1885.
- Soccer was on the official program of the 1904 Olympic Games in St. Louis. (The St. Rose and Christian Brothers teams of St. Louis competed; the Galt Football Club of Ontario, Canada, won the competition.)
- The United States competed in soccer at the 1924 Olympic Games in Paris.
- The United States placed third in the first World Cup soccer competition in 1930 at Montevideo, Uruguay. Uruguay defeated Argentina in the final round.
- Soccer outdrew all other sports at the 1984 Olympic Games in California. Two games drew more than 100,000 spectators.
- More than 8,000,000 players currently participate in American soccer.
- More than 1,000,000 soccer-oriented immigrants settle in the United States each year.
- Soccer crowds of 20,000 to 50,000 have been common in American sports stadiums during the past three decades.

Table 1.1 provides some idea of the sizes of American soccer crowds since 1977.

Table 1.1 The Twenty-One Largest Soccer Crowds in the United States

Aug. 11, 1984	France–2, Brazil–0	Rose Bowl	101,799
Aug. 10, 1984	Yugoslavia–2, Italy–1	Rose Bowl	100,374
Aug. 6, 1984	France–4, Yugoslavia–2	Rose Bowl	97,451
Aug. 8, 1984	Brazil–2, Italy–1	Stanford Stadium	83,642
July 29, 1984	U.S.–3, Costa Rica–0	Stanford Stadium	78,265
Aug. 14, 1977	Ft. Lauderdale vs. NY Cosmos	Giants Stadium	77,691
Oct. 1, 1977	Santos, Brazil vs. NY Cosmos	Giants Stadium	77,202
Aug. 7, 1982	Europe vs. World All-Stars	Giants Stadium	76,891
Aug. 29, 1979	Tulsa vs. NY Cosmos	Giants Stadium	76,031
Aug. 1, 1984	Brazil–1, W. Germany–0	Stanford Stadium	75,249
Aug. 27, 1978	Tampa Bay vs. NY Cosmos	Giants Stadium	74,901
Aug. 24, 1977	Rochester vs. NY Cosmos	Giants Stadium	73,669
Apr. 22, 1979	Ft. Lauderdale vs. NY Cosmos	Giants Stadium	72,342
May 21, 1978	Seattle vs. NY Cosmos	Giants Stadium	71,219
June 22, 1980	Ft. Lauderdale vs. NY Cosmos	Giants Stadium	70,312
Aug. 8, 1979	Tampa Bay vs. NY Cosmos	Giants Stadium	70,042
Aug. 5, 1984	Italy–1, Chile–0	Stanford Stadium	67,039
Aug. 5, 1984	France–2, Egypt–0	Rose Bowl	66,560
Aug. 23, 1978	Portland vs. NY Cosmos	Giants Stadium	65,287
May 30, 1984	Italy–0, U.S.–0	Giants Stadium	63,624
July 12, 1978	New England vs. NY Cosmos	Giants Stadium	62,497

Rules of the Game

2

FIFA (Federation of International Football Associations) laws are often modified at various levels to meet special needs, as can be seen from the "explanations" provided below. There are 17 rules of the game, which have been simplified in this chapter for easier understanding. Bear in mind, however, that these modified rules are just that: modified. The official laws of the game may be obtained by writing to the Federation of International Football Association (FIFA), Zurich, Switzerland.

Rule 1: The Playing Field

The rectangular field is at least 50 yards wide but no more than 80 yards. The minimum length is 100 yards, and the maximum 130 yards. At no time should the field be constructed into the dimensions of a square; the length should always exceed the width by a three-to-two ratio. The field has two *penalty areas,* two *goals,* a *center circle,* a *halfway line,* and four *corner-kick areas.* The penalty area has a *penalty spot* and a *goalkeeper area.* The sidelines are known as the *touchlines,* the end lines as the *goal lines.*

Explanation

The size of the field varies with the age of the players. Ideally it should be 74 yards by 112 yards. The National Collegiate Athletic Association (NCAA) calls for a minimum width of 65 yards (see Figure 2.1).

The penalty area is often referred to as the *penalty box.* It is 44 yards wide and 18 yards long.

The goal is centered on the goal line; the inside dimensions of the two posts and crossbar are 8 feet high by 24 feet wide. The goalposts should not be more than 5 inches wide and should not have any sharp prominences or anything that might alter the direction of the ball. The two posts perpendicular to the ground are also known as the *uprights,* and the connecting bar on top is known as the *crossbar.* The outside length of the crossbar is 24 feet 8 inches.

The *near post* is the goalpost on the same side of the field as the ball; the *far post* is on the opposite side. For example, if the ball is on the left side of the field, going in the direction of the opponents' goal, then the left goalpost is the near post and the right post is the far post. The goalposts and crossbar should be on, and directly over, the goal line, since they are part of the field of play; therefore, the lines of the field must not be more than 5 inches wide.

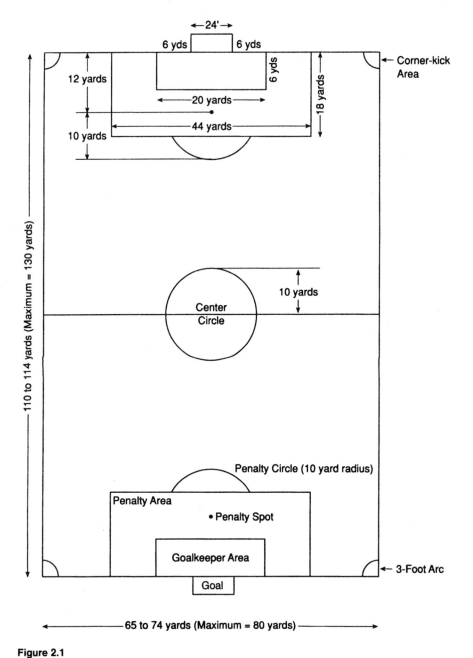

Figure 2.1
The playing field. Optimum size (as used in the World Cup Competition) is 74 yards by 112 yards.

A penalty spot is drawn 12 yards out from the middle of the goal on a line perpendicular to the goal line. The mark for the penalty spot should be 9 inches in diameter.

An arc is drawn and centered on the 18-yard line, which is the top of the penalty area. The arc has a 10-yard radius, using the penalty spot for the center. The arc is designed so that during a penalty kick, all players except the person taking the kick are at least 10 yards away from the ball at the moment the kick is taken. This assures each player an equal opportunity to replay the ball if it is deflected back into play by the goalie, the uprights, or the crossbar.

The center circle in the middle of the field is also drawn with a 10-yard radius. This keeps the defensive players from encroaching on the attackers when the game is started or restarted with a kickoff.

At each corner of the field, a one-yard radial arc is drawn from touchline to goal line, forming a quarter circle, with the corner as the center point. For a corner kick, the ball may be placed anywhere within this quarter circle. A corner flag is placed *directly on* the intersection of the lines at each corner of the field. These flags are considered part of the playing field, as are the goalposts and crossbar of each goal. At no time may a corner flag be removed during a game unless it has been damaged in such a way that it could prove dangerous to the players. The flag post must be solid but movable to prevent injury to a player who may collide with it, and it must be not less than 5 feet high. If the ball bounces off the corner flag back into play, or rests against it and is still inside or on the line, the ball is still in play.

The halfway line identifies the beginning of the offside area for the attacking team. Players in their defensive half of the field may never be called offside. (See Rule 11 for a definition of offside.)

The field should not have any dangerous holes, sprinklers, or anything that can, in the referee's opinion, endanger a player's safety. (See Rule 5 for definition of the referee.) There should be at least 10 feet between the touchline and any enclosing walls or hard surfaces; if such a condition is unavoidable, it must be made safe.

Rule 2: The Ball

The ball is a sphere covered with a rubber, leather, or leatherlike material approved by the FIFA. It should have no features that could injure the players. The circumference of the ball should be 27–28 inches and the weight should be 14–16 ounces.

Explanation

The ball size varies with the players' age. Boys and girls 8 years or younger may use a size 3 ball, which has a circumference of 22–23 inches. Children under the age of 13 may use a size 4 ball, which is 24–25 inches. Children over 13 and adults use a size 5 ball, which is 27–28 inches in circumference. The weight of a ball is proportional to the weight of the size 5 ball. The inflation pressure of the size 5 ball should be 10–12 pounds; the pressure of smaller balls is proportional. The ball should have various contrasting colored panels to increase its visibility and emphasize its spin.

Rule 3: Number of Players

Each team may have a maximum of 11 players and a minimum of 7 players on the field of play. A game is not considered valid if there are fewer than 7 players on either team. Both teams are allowed two substitutions during a game and may substitute whenever play stops. A substituted player, once off the field, may not come back on again for the rest of the game. A player who has been ejected prior to the start of the game may be replaced, but a player ejected during a game may not. (See Rule 12 regarding ejections.)

Explanation

At least 7 players per team must participate in an official contest. Thus, a game may be forfeited if more than 4 players on a team are ejected from a game or must leave because of injury, sickness, or for any other reason.

Rules about substitutions vary depending on the association or league and the level of competition. The number of substitutions that can be made during a single break in play is usually limited to two. When unlimited substitutions are allowed, the number of breaks is usually limited. In youth games, a substitution is only allowed when either team has a goal kick, a kickoff, or when the substituting team has a throw-in. For high school, college, or recreational leagues, rules for substituting vary and should be acknowledged by both teams before the game.

Rule 4: Equipment

Shorts, shirts, shin guards, socks, and shoes are mandatory. No player is allowed to wear rings, chains, or any other items that may be harmful to another player. The shoes should have cleats no longer than ½ inch, rounded, and with harmless flat tips. Goalies must have uniforms that distinguish them from the other players. For any infringement of this rule, the player will be sent off the field of play, until the situation has been corrected, and may not enter again until the referee has inspected the faulty equipment and given the player permission to reenter.

Explanation

Shoes are mandatory, but in areas of the world where living standards are marginal, the referee will allow play without footwear when all players are without shoes. Of course, most games are played with shoes and the players may wear any shoe they desire as long as the referee does not consider them dangerous.

Players may wear gloves or long pants beneath their uniforms, but only if all players on the team wear them. The only exception is the goalie, who alone may have gloves and padded pants, even if the others do not (some goalies also wear caps to keep the sun from their eyes). The equipment is acceptable only if it is not dangerous. Other allowances may be permitted if this guideline is observed.

The home team traditionally wears white. For the visiting team, contrasting colors are strongly recommended. On a green surface, this enhances the clarity of teams for spectators and helps players identify teammates' positions. Goalies must wear uniforms that contrast with their own teammates' uniforms as well as with those of the opponents. In the event of a color conflict, local league rules usually state that the home team will change colors.

Rule 5: The Referee

There is a referee and two linesmen who officiate a game. All three wear uniforms to distinguish them from the players. Their clothes consist of a solid black, short- or long-sleeve shirt, with white cuffs and white collar; solid black shorts; and black socks with white ribbing.

The referee is the head official. He or she is the judge of safe playing conditions; determines when trainers or coaches may enter the field; calls fouls; warns or suspends players if necessary; and may call off the game if it gets out of hand or if the weather becomes unsafe for play. The middle referee is the absolute officiator of the game and the one who keeps time and allows for extra playing time if the game is delayed or interrupted.

Explanation

Never argue, contradict, or even talk to the referee unless he or she talks to you. This, of course, does not include emergencies, and it refers to game time only. The team captain may inquire about the interpretation of calls made by a referee but only in a respectful manner. Swearing, which is categorized under the general heading of dissent, is not respectful and is penalized either with a caution or by ejection from the game without a second warning, at the referee's discretion. A player who receives two cautions in a game will be ejected.

Officials can only call what they see. All three officials have the same amount of authority, but the designated referee may overrule the two linesmen. Referees will, however, occasionally make mistakes since their angle of vision does not encompass everything. A good general practice is to *just "play the whistle."* This means to keep playing until the whistle is heard, rather than stop because you assume a foul was committed and a call is forthcoming. The time for any protest is after the game is over, and to the proper authorities, *not* to the referee. On rare occasions, associations have ordered games replayed and referees suspended for poor officiating.

Rule 6: The Linesmen

There are two linesmen to assist the referee. Their job is to signal, with a hand-held flag, when the ball is out of play and which side should receive possession for a goal kick, corner kick, or throw-in.

Explanation

The linesmen also signal for any fouls in their area that the referee did not see due to a poor angle of vision or being too far from the play. Their primary role is to stay even with the second to last defender and signal when and where an offensive player on their side of the field is offside (see Rule 11 for more about the second to last defender). This positioning allows maximum vision among the three officials.

Rule 7: Duration of The Game

There are two halves of 45 minutes each. The interval between halves is 5 minutes, unless the referee allows otherwise (e.g., in collegiate soccer, the interval is 10–15 minutes).

Explanation

A game may be called (terminated) if, in the judgment of the referee, the players are endangered. In poor weather conditions, the referee makes the final decision whether to continue play or stop the game. At the professional level, a ball dropping from 8 feet must bounce at least 8 inches on the playing field or the game cannot be played.

For younger players, the duration of the game varies with age. In case of a tied score, some organizations allow an overtime period; others do not. The FIFA orders two 15-minute overtime periods for *cup matches* (eliminatory competition: lose one game and the team is out). This is necessary when a winner must be determined, otherwise the game ends in a tie.

Rule 8: Start of Play

The winner of a coin toss, called by the captain of the visiting team, may choose either to kick off or to defend a certain end of the field. The referee will signal the beginning of the game by blowing a whistle. The ball is then kicked by the offensive team and must move, at least the distance of its circumference, into the opponents' half of the field before it is considered in play. The ball may not be retouched by the player who kicked off until someone else has touched it. After a goal has been scored and after half time, the game shall be restarted in the same manner but without the coin toss. After a goal, the team that has been scored on kicks off to restart the game. To start a new half, the team that did not kick off first will switch sides and have the kickoff. All players must be on their own half of the field at the kickoff, and the defending team must stay out of the center circle until the ball has first been kicked. A goal may not be scored directly from a kickoff.

For any temporary suspension of the game not specified by the rules, the referee shall restart the game by dropping the ball where it was when the game was stopped. Players may not kick the ball until it touches the ground. If a drop ball is called for while the ball is in the goal area, it will be dropped *outside* the goal area, at a point equal in distance from the goal line and nearest to its spot when play was suspended. Any infringement will result in the ball being re-dropped, unless the kicker plays the ball again before it is played by anyone else; in this case an indirect kick will be awarded to the opposing team from the spot of the infraction. If a foul is committed before the ball hits the ground, the player will be cautioned or ejected, depending on the seriousness of the foul, and the ball will be redropped. If the ball goes out of bounds or through the goal before a second player touches it, it will be redropped.

Rule 9: Ball in or out of Play

The ball is out of play when:

a. It is *entirely* over the touchline or goal line, meaning that a perpendicular tangent to the ball does not touch the width of the line. (See Figure 2.2.)
b. The game is stopped by the referee.

The ball is otherwise in play even if:

a. It rebounds from a goalpost, crossbar, or corner flag and back onto the field of play.
b. It rebounds off the referee, a linesman, or a spectator, when they are on the field of play.

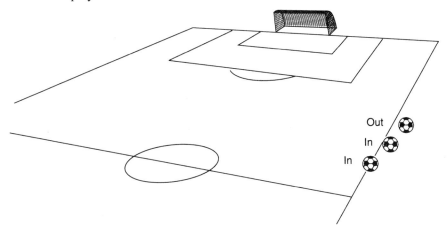

Figure 2.2
The ball is in play as long as it *touches* the four-inch wide touchline.

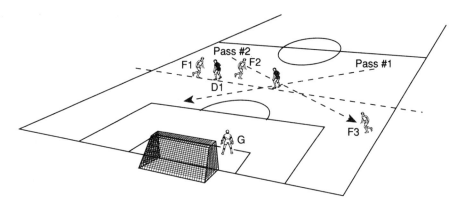

Figure 2.3
Rule 11: Offside.

Rule 10: Scoring

A goal is scored when the *whole* ball crosses entirely over the goal line between the posts and under the crossbar. It is not a goal if the ball is flat or exploding as it goes into the goal. A goal may not be scored directly from an indirect free kick, a throw-in, a goal kick, or a kickoff.

Rule 11: Offside

An attacker who is ahead of the ball and nearer to the opponents' goal line than at least two defenders when the ball is passed (the goalie counting as one) is in an *offside* position, unless the attacker is in his or her own half of the field an attacking player can be on the same line with the last defender and not be offside (not counting the goalie). The attacker will be penalized for being in an offside position if the referee determines that at the moment the ball was played by a teammate, the attacker had gained an advantage and/or was interfering with the play. A player cannot be offside during a corner kick, a throw-in, a goal kick, or a drop ball.

In Figure 2.3, player F1 is not offside at the time a pass is made, since he or she is on the same imaginary line as D1. In the case of pass # 1, however, the referee may decide that F3 is not offside since F3 is not in a position to interfere with the play. In the case of pass # 2, F3 is considered offside. In the case of either pass, player F2 is not offside.

Rule 12: Fouls and Misconduct

A foul is committed when a player kicks, trips, jumps at, violently charges, strikes, spits at, holds, or pushes another player, or intentionally handles the ball with any part of the arm or hand. In this case, a *direct* free kick is awarded to the opposing team. Play is stopped and restarted where the offense occurred. (See Rule 13 for direct and indirect free kicks.)

An *indirect* free kick is awarded to the opposing team if:

- a player engages in playing in a dangerous or violent manner;
- a player charges fairly with the shoulder but does not play the ball, or if the ball is not within playing distance;
- a player intentionally obstructs an opponent;
- a player charges the goalie while the goalie is inside his or her goal area;
- the goalie, after gaining control of the ball with his or her hands, takes more than four steps to release the ball back into play;
- the goalie puts the ball down and picks it up again directly or from a teammate while both are still in the penalty area (18-yard box).

A player will be given a caution (yellow card) for:

- discourteous conduct (extremely dangerous or violent play);
- dissent (foul or abusive language or gestures);
- persistent infringement of the rules of the game;
- entering or leaving the field during play without the referee's permission;
- for tactical and intentional fouls.

A player will be ejected from the game (given a red card) for:

- violent conduct or serious foul play;
- extremely foul or abusive language or gestures;
- persistent misconduct after receiving a caution (two cautions [yellow cards] equals an ejection [red card]);
- foul on a player in scoring position.

Explanation

The following are examples of dangerous play:

- When the ball is at *head* level and one player heads it while an opposing player tries to kick it; the player attempting to kick the ball is endangering the player heading it and thus is called for the foul.
- When the ball at is *waist* level and one player kicks it while the other player tries to head it; the player attempting to head it is endangering himself and thus is called for the foul.

When a player receives a caution, the referee will indicate this to the teams, coaches, and spectators by holding a yellow card above his or her head. The referee will also make written note of the caution in a notebook.

If a player is ejected, the referee will hold a red card above the player's head. In this case the player must leave the field of play, including the sidelines, and may not enter again for the duration of the game. In addition, the player's team must play one person short for the rest of the game. After the game, the incident is reported to a proper sanctioning board, which will decide on further punishment, depending on the seriousness of the offense. Usually the player is suspended from competing in the next match.

Only players and coaches may be cautioned or ejected. However, if spectators become too unruly, the referee may caution the team or coach, or may terminate the game.

Rule 13: Free Kicks

There are two types of free kicks: *direct* and *indirect*. When either kick is taken, all opposing players must be at least 10 yards away. If a player encroaches (moves closer than 10 yards) and then blocks the kick, the kick shall be retaken.

Explanation

The difference between a direct kick and an indirect kick is that a goal may be scored *directly* from a direct kick. For a goal to be scored from an indirect kick, the ball must be touched by a second player (from either team) before it enters the goal. Hence a goal may be scored only *indirectly* from an indirect free kick. The referee will signal for an indirect free kick by raising an arm straight above the head. For a direct free kick, the referee will only indicate the direction of the kick.

Free kicks account for many scores, especially when they are awarded within 30 yards of the goal. A good offensive player will try to draw a foul in this area. Because of the high probability of the offensive team scoring from a free kick taken near the goal, the defensive team will usually make a human wall of players between the ball and the goal. Thus, if the offensive player elects to shoot the ball directly, it must go around or over the wall, making it harder to score. The number of players in the defensive wall varies with the angle and distance from the goal and the spot where the ball is placed. The closer and more centered the ball is on the goal, the more people are placed in the wall.

The defending team may stand no closer than 10 yards from the ball until it has been kicked. A goal may be scored directly from a corner kick. If the player taking the kick touches it a second time before anyone else does, an indirect free kick will be awarded to the opposing team where the offending player last touched it. For any other infringement, the kick will be retaken.

Rule 14: Penalty Kicks

If a foul resulting in a direct kick is committed by the defensive team in its 18-yard box (the *penalty box* or *penalty area*), a penalty kick will be awarded to the offensive team. In this case, all players except the person taking the kick (who need not be the player fouled) must stand outside the penalty box and arc. The ball is placed on the penalty spot, which is centered on the goal and 12 yards from the goal line. The goalie must stand on the goal line and may not move his or her feet off the line until the ball is kicked. If the penalty kick rebounds into the field of play from an upright or the crossbar, without touching the goalie, the kicker may not replay the ball until it touches someone else. If the defensive team infringes on any part of this rule but a goal is not scored, the kick will be retaken. If the offensive team infringes on any part of this rule and scores a goal, the goal will be disallowed and play restarted with a goal kick for the defensive team.

Rule 15: Throw-Ins

When the whole of the ball passes over a touchline (sideline), either on the ground or in the air, it must be thrown in from where the ball went out of bounds. The player must have both feet in contact with the ground and one at least partially on the touchline through the entire motion of the throw. The ball may be thrown in any direction, but it must be thrown with both hands evenly, and the throw must begin from behind the head. The ball is in play the moment it crosses the plane of the touchline. If the ball lands out of bounds (a possibility on extremely windy days) without entering play, the throw will be retaken by the same team from the same spot. The player throwing the ball may not touch the ball again until someone else has touched it. Any infringement of this rule will result in a throw-in by the opposing team. If the ball is thrown directly into the goal without being touched by another player, the result will be a goal kick taken by the opposing team.

Rule 16: Goal Kicks

When the entire ball crosses the goal line—but not between the two goalposts—and was last touched by the *attacking* team, a goal kick shall be taken by the defending team to restart play. The ball may be placed anywhere in the half of the goal area toward the point where the ball went out. In other words, if the ball goes out to the left of the goal, it may be placed anywhere within the left half of the goal area. After the kick, the ball may not be played by either team until it has passed out of the penalty area. If it is played a second time inside the penalty area, the kick will be retaken.

If the kicker touches the ball a second time after it passes out of the penalty area and before someone else touches it, an indirect free kick will be awarded to the opposing team at the spot where the offending player last touched the ball. All opposing players must remain outside the penalty area until the ball has cleared that area. A goal may not be scored directly from a goal kick.

Rule 17: Corner Kicks

When the entire ball crosses the goal line (but not between the two goalposts) and was last touched by the *defending* team, a corner kick shall be taken by the attacking team to restart play. The ball may be placed anywhere in the corner area corresponding to the side of the goal the ball went out on. The flag may not be moved. The kicker may not play the ball again until it has been touched by another player.

Basic Techniques

3

As a chain is no stronger than its weakest link, the soccer team depends upon each player's ability to master the fundamentals: trapping, dribbling, kicking, passing, shooting, tackling, heading, and throw-ins.

Trapping

Inside of the foot. The most common type of trap for a slow ground ball is with the inside of the foot. One foot supports the body weight while the other, a few inches away from the supporting foot, meets and stops the ball while drawing the foot back a couple of inches to soften the impact. (See Figure 3.1.)

Sole of the foot. Trapping with the sole of the foot is for high, gently sloped balls due to land forward of the weight-carrying foot. If the left foot carries the weight, the ball should land approximately one foot to the right and one foot forward. The right knee is slightly bent; the toe and the heel form a 45-degree angle with the ground. (See Figure 3.2a.) The heel is no more than four to five inches above the playing surface, forming a natural angle with the toe, which acts as a shock absorber. Do not step on the ball or bring the foot up higher than the diameter of the ball; on wet surfaces, the ball could, depending upon its flight angle, skip and slide under your foot. (See Figure 3.2b.) The player must estimate where the ball will land and cover that spot on impact as described above.

Figure 3.1
Trapping with the inside of the foot.

Figure 3.2a
Cover the spot where the ball will land. The heel should not be higher from the ground than the diameter of the ball.

Figure 3.2b
Allowing the ball to bounce on a wet or slippery surface may lead to loss of control.

If the sole meets the ball only slightly, covering about one-fourth of the ball's diameter, then the ball will thrust forward a few feet. This variation, the *running toe trap,* has its uses when a fast, forward run is necessary. (See Figure 3.3.)

Thigh trap. If a high lofted ball is falling diagonally toward the midsection of the body, the player should move to meet it with the lower or upper part of the thigh (see Figures 3.4 and 3.5). Using the lower part causes a slow, forward bounce; using the upper part will stop it completely. In the latter trap, the knee is elevated about one foot higher than its normal position.

Figure 3.3
The running toe trap. The ball will dart forward as it meets the foot.

Figure 3.4
The lower-thigh trap.

Figure 3.5
The upper-thigh trap.

Figure 3.6
Trapping a high ball with the chest. The hands are kept wide for balance.

Chest trap. The chest trap is used for high balls, coming at sloping angles above the midsection of the body, or fast, straight, chest-high balls. (See Figure 3.6.) For higher balls, the upper part of the body is bent slightly back to meet the ball on the upper part of the chest. As the ball touches the chest, the player quickly draws back a few inches. This decelerates and cradles the ball so it will not bounce away. The upper arms are held wide and at an angle to the lower arms, which should be pointing up and away from the ball. Turning the body to the right or to the left as it meets the ball will help redirect the ball in one motion.

This trap keeps the ball above the waistline and prevents an opponent from kicking it away, which would be whistled as a dangerous play.

When a ball comes fast and chest high, almost parallel to the ground, the upper part of the body is bent forward to meet it on the middle part of the thoracic area, about 8 inches below the neck. The ball will be deflected to the ground at the player's feet.

Side-of-the-foot trap. The side-of-the-foot trap is used for a medium high ball that would meet the ground slightly to the side and behind the weight-carrying foot. The trapping foot should be almost perpendicular to the supporting foot. The knee should be bent forward and slightly inward over the space where the ball will be stopped. The distance between the feet should be no more than the ball's diameter and the heel-to-toe line of the trapping foot should be parallel to the ground. (See Figure 3.7.)

Dribbling

The player should push the ball forward with the inside of the foot, using both feet and making sure the ball is no more than 3 feet away. The outside of the foot should not be used except in practice dribbling drills because an unanticipated tackle may cause the dribbler to roll over an ankle, causing permanent damage.

Figure 3.7
Side-of-the-foot trap.

Figure 3.8
Dribbling while looking ahead of the ball. © James L. Shaffer

From an early age, a player should learn to push the ball gently forward, alternating feet as necessary and keeping the ball close. At this point, the player should also be taught to *keep looking 6 to 10 feet ahead of the ball.* (See Figure 3.8.) This will help the player learn to use his or her peripheral vision and to pay attention to what takes place in the field ahead.

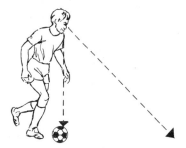

Figure 3.9
Dribbling with the head bent slightly forward and the eyes focused ahead. The ball is kept close
to the feet and struck with alternating feet.

Players must also be made aware of the correct body position as they move
with the ball. They should run mostly on the balls of the feet, heels off the ground,
body tilted slightly forward. The head should also be bent slightly forward so
that the cheekbones do not obstruct vision of the ball. (See Figure 3.9.)

Warmup sessions should include as much dribbling as possible. During practices, dribbling should not be limited to straight lines, but should include zigzag
patterns, as when trying to get free of a crowded area in a game. This forces
players to keep the ball close and become aware of opposing players around them.
The idea is to *look for space and go to it.*

Various limitations should be imposed during drills to enhance particular
dribbling skills, such as:

• using the right foot only;
• using the left foot only;
• using alternate feet;
• using the outside of the foot only;
• alternating the outside and inside of the right and left foot in sequence.

This constant change develops the players' concentration, improves their skills,
and adds variety and interest to the drills.

Kicking

The ball may be kicked with the outside, inside, instep, toe, heel, or the inner
edge of the foot. In kicking, the player should be aware that there are two primary motions as contact is made with the ball; the swing of the thigh and the
swing of the foot from the knee. These two motions together account for the total
power of the kick. Most of the power comes from the snap of the foot by the knee.
Like a whip handle, the thigh begins the swing of the leg; as the knee becomes
centered directly above the ball, the foot—with the heel almost touching the back
of the thigh—is released and snapped into the ball.

Figure 3.10
Kicking for height.

Figure 3.11
Kicking with the outside of the foot.

The toe of the nonkicking foot should always be pointing toward the intended target. This allows the hips, and thus the body, to be properly lined up in the direction of the kick. The eyes must watch the ball all the way through the kick, so that proper contact between foot and ball can be made.

The placement of the nonkicking foot will affect the height of the ball's flight. Usually when the nonkicking foot is farther away from and slightly in back of the ball, and the body is leaning back and away from it, the ball will go higher in the air. (See Figure 3.10.) When the nonkicking foot is even alongside the ball, the body is leaning over it, causing the ball to stay low in its trajectory. Further, if the arch of the kicking foot makes contact underneath the ball, the ball will pop up in the air; if the arch makes contact above the middle of the ball, the ball will be forced downward. If the foot strikes the ball at mid-level, the height of the ball will not be altered.

Outside of the foot. In kicking with the outside of the foot, the outside area of the kicking foot next to the shoelace meets the center of the ball. (See Figure 3.11.) As the foot meets the ball, the ankle is stiff and the toe extended down and inward toward the nonkicking foot. The nonkicking foot should be placed slightly in back of the ball. When the ball is kicked, its spin will cause it to move in the direction away from the side it was struck on. This type of kick is dangerous. If the ball is blocked by an opponent, the player can sprain an ankle.

Instep. The instep or "shoelace" kick is the most powerful of all. The ball can travel over 130 miles per hour. The toe should be down, ankle stiff, heel and toe in line with the direction of the kick. The kicking foot's angle to the ball will affect the ball's flight. If the foot strikes the center section of the ball, the ball will go low; if it strikes the bottom half, it will go high. If the foot strikes the ball off-center to the right, the ball will go left, and vice versa. The nonkicking foot should be placed near and even with the ball as it is kicked. (See Figures 3.12 and 3.13.)

Figure 3.12
Instep kick. Side and back view position of feet. Note the position of the nonkicking foot.

Figure 3.13
Another view of the instep kick. Note the position of the nonkicking foot.

Figure 3.14a
Inside edge of the foot.

Toe and heel kicks. In toe and heel kicks, the foot forms a 90-degree angle with the lower leg when viewed from the side. The ankle is again stiff. With a gentle swing, the toe or heel strikes the center of the ball (if it is struck off-center, its course will be badly misdirected). The motion is quick and hard to anticipate, which is why it is effective at catching an opponent offguard. To keep the element of surprise, both kicks should be used sparingly. Caution is advised with the heel kick because an opponent attempting a tackle may miss the ball and hurt the unprotected Achilles tendon. Some shin guards provide a little protection for the tendon, but more improvements are needed in this area of equipment.

Inside edge of the foot (inner edge of the shoelaces). These kicks are among the most common. The toe is pointed down and slightly outward so that the heel points inward. The ankle is only partially extended and stiff. As the ball is struck, it will have a spin that will cause it to curve to the side opposite the one it was struck on. The nonkicking foot is slightly behind and diagonally away from the ball when it is kicked. Use the inside edge of the foot for long, high passes in crosses. (See Figure 3.14a.)

Inside of the foot. When kicking with the inside of the foot, the foot should meet the center of the ball, at the area where the shin meets the foot. The toe and the heel are roughly parallel to the ground (the toe may be somewhat elevated above the heel), allowing the foot to be close to the playing surface. The toe of the kicking foot should turn gently inward *as it follows through* so that it is pointing toward the intended target—the same direction the nonkicking foot is pointed. The nonkicking foot should be even with the ball as it is kicked. (See Figure 3.14b.)

This type of kick is the most accurate, and thus the most used, since the maximum foot area makes contact with the ball. The more foot surface area is used, the more control a player has over the ball.

Chip. The chip is used to loft the ball with backspin, so that it floats in the air and drops softly without rolling too fast. Backspin on a long, high pass slows the bounce of the ball. The higher the ball, the more time it takes to come down, making it possible for a runner to get to it. (See Figure 3.14c.)

Figure 3.14b
Inside of the foot kick.

Figure 3.14c
Chip.

The chip is used to send a ball over a defender. Place the nonkicking foot alongside the ball. The ankle of the kicking foot should be stiff, with the toe at about 90 degrees, pointing forward. The ball should be struck centrally and from underneath, so that the sole of the foot brushes along the ground, like a wedge between the ball and the ground.

Passing

Passing is kicking at a target. Factors to consider are distance, accuracy, velocity, and timing. These in turn depend upon whether the target is moving or stationary, the positioning of opponents, and the passer's intentions. (This subject is discussed further in Chapter 7 under "The Meaning of a Pass.")

The most accurate and most common is the *inside-of-the-foot* pass. Like the inside-of-the-foot kick, it is the most accurate because the maximum area of the foot makes contact with the ball. Although it is not very powerful, for most soccer passes only a short to medium range is required, up to 30 yards along the ground. For longer distances, 30–40 yards in the air, the *inside-edge-of-the-arch* pass is used. Like the corresponding kick, this pass will bend away from the side the ball was struck on. This makes it very convenient when an attacking passer is playing the ball across the width of the field (a *cross pass*) and wants the ball to bend away from a goalie or defender and into the path of a teammate. This type of pass can be given backspin, to slow the bounce of a long forward pass.

The *outside of the foot* can be used for short or long passes. The ball will curve inward and then outward. Players should exercise caution in curving a ball; if the ball is hit too full, it will be way off-target. The outside-of-the-foot pass is convenient for bending the ball outward to a teammate or around the goalie.

The *instep* is rarely used for passes. The area of the foot that strikes the ball is so small that it is easy to hit off-target. However, if the player is skilled and speed and distance are needed, then this is the pass to use.

In most long passes, the ball is hit below its middle and has backspin. This slows the ball in the air and also when it hits the ground. If a forward bounce is needed, then a *high instep* (shoelace) pass should be used. The passer places the nonkicking foot away from and behind the ball and strikes the ball in the middle, leaning back and away from it.

Toe and heel passes are rarely expected and are used mainly as a surprise tactic. When a player is close to the goal and has no time to wind up and shoot, a quick toe "punch" can be an effective shot. Remember, however, that the heel and toe kick is not precise because of the small surface area of the foot that makes contact with the ball.

Shooting

Shooting requires power and speed, which are most often achieved by using the instep (shoelace), outer or inner instep, and arch areas. Power comes from a full swing of the lower leg together with a full swing of the thigh. It is important that the thigh and foot follow through after contact with the ball is made. As noted in the section on kicking, the toe should be down, the ankle stiff, and the thigh extended back as far as possible with the leg bent at the knee.

Early on, players should develop facility in shooting with both feet, since in a game situation there is often no time to switch to the favored foot.

The objective is to hit the ball hard, low, and in the direction of the goal. This way, even if the ball does not go into the goal, there is a good chance that either a defender or the goalie will deflect it into the back of the goal for a score, or that it will rebound, giving a teammate an opportunity to shoot.

If the ball is shot high or wide of the goal, it will merely go out of bounds, with no further chance to score and loss of possession as well. All the effort put into advancing the ball downfield and into a scoring position is thus wasted because of poor shooting technique.

Figure 3.15a
Tackling the ball (front view).

Figure 3.15b
Tackling the ball (side view).

Tackling

When a defender tries to stop the progress of an opponent in possession of the ball, the defender is said to be "tackling" the opponent. To tackle, the opponent must be forced into a one-on-one situation and timing is important. The tackling player should "jockey," that is, delay the opponent, making a move to steal the ball only when he or she feels close enough to win it. (See Figure 3.15a and b.)

The classic way to tackle either a 50–50 ball (a ball not clearly in the possession of either opposing player) or one in possession of an opposing player is with the inside of the foot. The foot used should be the one nearest the opponent. If the back leg were lifted and swung at the ball, a skilled opponent would see it coming and push the ball by the tackler. The tackler, having stopped to make the tackle, would then be helpless to keep the opponent from going by. It takes much less time to make a tackle with the near foot, giving the opponent less chance to react.

For protection from the opponent's body, the tackler's forearm should be parallel to the ground and about 6 inches from the abdomen. The upper body leans slightly forward, allowing for some shoulder-to-shoulder contact when the adversary does the same thing for a 50–50 ball. The body should be used as a wall to block the ball and make it bounce behind the opponent. Do not tackle by merely kicking at the ball because it is likely that the ball will bounce off the opponent and continue to go his or her way.

Slide tackle. Sometimes a tackling player can slide into the ball, block it, and push it away with the sole of the sliding foot. The obvious advantage of slide tackling is that it throws the whole force of the body's weight and speed behind the ball. However, if the timing is bad, the opponent who sees the tackle coming can easily dribble away. Once on the ground, the tackler cannot recover fast enough to get back into the play, leaving the attacker with a clear break toward the goal.

When running alongside an opponent who has the ball, the defender may legally use a shoulder to "charge" the ball carrier. But there is a fine line between a legal "nudge" and an illegal one. The important rule to remember is that, when tackling from the front side, or behind, the player must make solid contact with the ball first, not by going "through" the opponent's body. This rule makes it difficult to win tackles legally, but it can be done with patience and with plenty of practice in timing and proper technique.

Heading

In heading, only the forehead should make contact with the ball. A ball that hits anywhere else on the head is harder to control and is painful. The eyes must be kept open during the entire incoming flight of the ball (the eyes may blink at the time of impact). Otherwise, it is not unlikely that the ball will hit the player in the nose or that the player will mishead it. The feet should be firmly planted on the ground with one foot (it does not matter which one) slightly behind the other.

In heading the ball from a standing position, the strength of the header comes from the waist. The upper body should cock back, with the chin slightly tucked in and the eyes following the ball. (See Figure 3.16.) The arms should be bent at the elbows so that the forearms are parallel to the ground and facing the direction of the ball. This is to give balance and to help the player avoid being pushed out of the ball's path.

As the ball reaches the space where the head would normally be—that is, the space directly above the feet on the ground—the player should release the upper body and snap the forehead into the ball. At the same time, the forearms should be pulled back to add speed and strength to the header. Be sure that the neck is extended out and into the ball and not tucked into the chest.

For a jumping header, the technique is the same except that, as the upper body cocks back, the heels should pull up to the buttocks and, as the upper body snaps forward into the ball, the feet should be kicked forward as well.

When trying to head a ball approaching from an angle, the player should jump off the foot closer to the ball. The knee of the outside foot is brought up and around, rotating the body in the air and bringing it directly into line with the path of the ball.

Figure 3.16
This player is preparing to head the ball. Note the hands held wide for balance (right foreground).

When attempting to head a ball on goal from a cross path from the right side of the field, the left side of the body should be positioned toward the goal. The ball should make contact with the center or the left side of the forehead. When the ball is headed, the motion of the body should redirect it toward the goal. For a cross from the left side of the field, the right side of the body should be angled toward the goal. A pendulum—a ball hanging from a cord placed at various heights can be used for individual technique.

Throw-ins

In a throw-in, the ball is held by both hands with the thumbs behind the ball. It is brought back all the way behind the head with the arms and then thrown forward evenly by both hands. If the ball is not brought back all the way behind the head or if it has a side spin on it, it will be considered a foul throw and be rethrown by the opposing team.

Both feet must be touching the ground at the moment the ball is released. The feet may be together if throwing from a standstill, or they may be one in front of the other if throwing from a run. In a running throw-in, the back foot remains on the ground at release by dragging the toe. The body must face the direction of the throw and the throw must be executed in one fluid motion. (See Figure 3.17.)

In training players for longer throws, the "overload principle" can be used. A 6- to 7-pound medicine ball can be used for practicing powerful short throws. When the lighter soccer ball is substituted, the distance of the throw will increase.

Figure 3.17
The throw-in. Note that the toe of the rear foot is in contact with the ground at the moment the ball is released from above and behind the head.

Restarts

Any deadball situation—when the referee stops the game for fouls, corner kicks, throw-ins, or goal kicks—is considered a *restart*. These situations account for about 70 percent of goal-scoring, so set plays for restart situations should be well rehearsed.

Throw-ins may be considered goal scoring opportunities when they occur near the opponents' goal, especially since the offside rule is not in effect on a throw-in. Players who can make long throw-ins—that is, from the touchline to the area in front of the opponent's goal—should be used in conjunction with players who are strong on heading.

On direct and indirect free kicks taken 30 yards or less from the goal, the defenders may be expected to form a human wall. A second whistle is not required to restart the game, so the element of surprise should be cultivated. In other words, the attackers should take the kick quickly, if possible before the wall is completely formed. Most of the time, a wall of 2–5 players is used, depending on the shooting angle and proximity of the ball to the goal. (See Figure 3.18.) The greater the angle to the goal or the further the distance from the goal, the fewer players are needed in the wall. If an indirect free kick is taken inside the penalty area, a wall of up to 10 players (11 if the wall is on the goal line) may be formed. (See Figure 3.19.)

Corner kicks may involve a multitude of set plays, such as near-post runs, short chips, hard-driven shots, or just playing the ball back to retain possession and initiate a new attack.

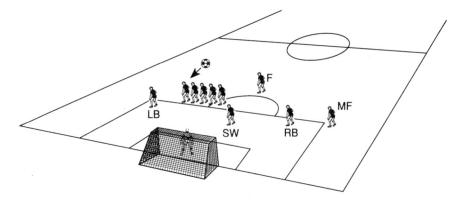

Figure 3.18

The defensive team forms a wall to protect against a direct kick. SW–Sweeper covering back of wall; RB–Right back; LB–Left back; MF/F–Midfield or Forward ready to block shot from lateral pass.

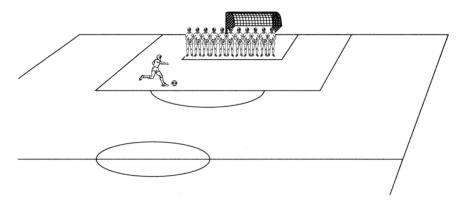

Figure 3.19

Indirect free kick inside the penalty area. If the kick is from 10 yards out or less, all players must cover the goal *mouth* by placing themselves on the goal line. Players cannot move until the ball is kicked.

Player Development

4

Player Preparation

For players under the age of 12, training is primarily geared to entertain and to teach fundamentals. The game should be fun.

Training may start at 6 or 7 years of age with 7 players playing on small fields one-quarter the size of a regulation field. Small goals should be used. The smaller field allows more contact with the ball and less running around. Contact with the ball is what makes the game fun.

At the age of 10 or 11, full teams can be formed on fields about two-thirds of the regular size, 80 by 55 yards. From 11 to 14, fields of 100 by 65 yards are recommended. After 14, players should use regular 112- by 74-yard fields.

Quality coaching is necessary from the beginning to ensure that basic techniques are learned correctly. By the age of 12, sound fundamentals should be pretty well established: basic ball control, ability to use both feet, ability to move for space and back up a teammate, one or two dribbling moves, correct heading, ability to cover a player when defending, and familiarity with basic rules like fouls and offsides. Once they have these basic skills, players can maintain and polish them and start learning the tactical aspects of the game.

About 10 months of competition are needed for development, with a game every week and 3 practices between games. This provides sufficient rest before and after games and enough practice time to correct mistakes and learn to prepare for the next contest. Every game is a learning situation. Once mistakes are exposed, correct techniques must be practiced. *Simply knowing that a mistake was made will not break a bad habit.* The player needs time for the new knowledge to sink in.

Games should be reasonably difficult and challenging. Approximately 40 games per year will slowly mold the player. After about 40 years of coaching, I estimate that in this country we need about 400 good, challenging games to develop a player by the age of 18.

Bad habits will persist when the opposition is weak. Strong competition for 15- to 16-year-olds will bring out the best in each player. Young people at this age should play with their peers, not against older players. They are still developing and, if the competition is too strong, they will do whatever they can to survive and not try anything new. Players who become afraid of failure will not develop. However, if the challenge of the game encourages them to attempt and perfect new plays or fakes, they may become very good.

Continuity in coaching and coaching philosophy is also very important. Changing coaches every two or three years is not bad if the new coach has the same basic philosophy and an approach similar to his or her predecessor's. Before taking charge, the new coach should know the players and their capabilities and shortcomings. The coach should keep records of each player's strengths and weaknesses, as well as morphology.

While growing, the young player should be checked for morphological problems. A sports medicine doctor should be available for consultation on these, as well as on any unexpected problems. Inadequate lung capacity; weak back, hips, or ankles; loose knees; or just inadequately developed muscle groups can hamper soccer players. With proper help, these deficiencies can be corrected. After the age of 16, weight training designed to increase strength and endurance should be available.

The coach deals with the person within, not just the player. He or she should know the player's family and be aware when outside factors may affect a player's performance. Effort should be made to assure that each player has the necessary positive support. Parental cooperation is very helpful, if not essential. All players should not be treated the same; some need more attention than others and have varied levels of sensitivity. Each must be motivated to have confidence and reach his or her best. Winning is only a necessary evil; there is no such thing as a lost game when a lesson is learned from it. The score does not always reflect the full outcome of the game.

In training players, different surfaces should be used whenever available. Clay, grass, and Astroturf fields, both wet and dry, accustom the player to the characteristics of various surfaces.

Above all, the head coach should always be present at practice to direct and monitor the activities.

Equipment and Exercises

Care should be exercised in selecting the right shoes and equipment. Moderately priced shoes, properly fit, are the most desirable. Soccer is an all-weather game so a wind- and water-resistant training suit is necessary. Reversible cotton T-shirts are practical for training purposes, but colored bibs can be just as effective. The old gray cotton sweatsuit is still the best for long wear and abuse. Shin guards should be introduced at an early age so players can become used to them. Every player should own several appropriately sized practice balls and a few cones, to be used when they practice on their own.

Running takes time away from practice, so players should do most of it on their own time and use practice sessions to maintain their condition. When with their coach, players should learn things like tactics, teamwork, and skill. Most *individual* technical drills can be practiced by kicking a ball against a wall or by practicing certain traps or kicks (for at least 30 minutes a day). Ball kicking for precision is readily developed by players who, on their own time, practice drills such as the following.

Two sets of cones are placed 20 yards apart, forming two small goals, each 6 feet wide. Kick five balls from one goal to the other, then jog to the other area and kick them back toward the first goal. Do not gather the balls; kick them toward the other goal from where they landed. Fifty shots each should be taken with the instep, with the side of the foot, and as high, lofted passes. Repeating this cycle with the opposite foot makes for a total of 300 kicks. Persistence in this training will make the individual's accuracy close to perfect. In game situations it makes for pinpoint passing. Since it is time-consuming, players should do this on their own time. Any deficiency should be spotted early and specific individual training prescribed. (A training center with all the necessary equipment could facilitate this type of work.)

A helpful aid is the "pit," which is a 30- by 30-yard square surrounded by a 14-foot wall. Here, the player shoots from the middle to a make-believe goal. As it rebounds, he or she shoots again at a make-believe goal on one or the other walls. This teaches the player to receive the ball and turn to shoot right or left. This training device is seldom found in the average neighborhood, so look for available practice tennis courts that have two or three walls and can serve the same purpose. More shots can be taken in ten minutes in the pit or practice tennis court than in hours of game or practice time.

Many other devices can aid player preparation. Some of the devices below are somewhat uncommon, but any suitable substitute will suffice.

- Any wall can be used for all-around skill improvement.
- Cones may be used for making grids, goals, obstacles for slalom dribbling etc. Ideally they are 14 inches high.
- A partner is helpful for a variety of conditioning drills, for example, getting down on all fours for the other partner to jump back and forth over.
- The jump rope is useful for leg muscle strength, coordination, and cardiovascular development.
- Weight training helps build strength and some bulk.
- The "tunnel" is an enclosed area 20–30 yards long with padding at the end, used for precision power shooting.
- The "pendulum"—a ball hanging from a cord—can be used for improving the jump and timing of a head ball.
- The medicine ball is used overhead to develop the upper body muscles necessary for long throw-ins and goalie throws.
- Videotaping performance makes it possible to review individual mistakes, note correct execution, and otherwise observe performance.
- The circuit training course includes a number of stations that incorporate some of the devices listed above, such as the medicine ball and the jump rope.

Skill Development

In essence, *soccer "skill" is technique under pressure*. A 95 percent rate of accuracy in execution is the ideal for all basic skills. This is achieved by starting with simple tasks, such as trapping the ball at the feet, using one or two touches on the ball to control it, and passing the ball with 100 percent accuracy, to a teammate who is not moving. These basic techniques are then expanded to form more complex skills.

While becoming proficient in the basics, such as passing and trapping, the player persistently works toward more complicated technique, like trapping the ball away from a defending player and *into* an open space 3 to 6 yards away, thus creating time to pass, dribble, or shoot the ball. Another example of higher-level skill is passing the ball to the space toward which a teammate is running, so that he or she can meet the ball without having to break stride. With such incremental training, time will take over and do its magic.

Constant rehearsal is needed to maintain what has been learned while concentrating on improvement. The overall goal is always faster, better execution while *under pressure*. In teaching technique, however, proper execution is much more important than speed. The practice of correct reactions during training leads to proper reactions in a game. Thus it is important to conduct every drill and exercise under game conditions.

As an example, we will look at "complicated" drills that combine passing, dribbling, and/or shooting, with the intention of scoring a goal by moving the ball from position A to its final destination through the goal. These drills are deemed complicated because they involve many parts, an error in any one of which will delay progress and weaken the whole.

Of course, we all make mistakes, so why the fuss? Let's say we have a "set piece" (any *dead ball* situation with immediate goal-scoring potential, such as a corner kick or an offensive free kick within 30 yards of the goal) involving 5 players. Each player is to receive a pass, control it, and pass to another player before shooting the ball.

If the individual margin of error is 20 percent for each player, there is a 100 percent chance of failure (5 players by 20 percent). If the margin of error is only 10 percent, then 50 percent of all attempts will fail. A 5 percent margin of error results in a 25 percent error factor, meaning that one in every four plays will fail. With a 2.5 percent margin of error, 12.5 percent, or one out of every eight plays, will fail. A 25 percent error factor is fair, but 12.5 percent is the desired goal for proficiency in complicated tasks. This means that each player's margin of error is only 1–3 percent.

Players often want to attempt advanced tactical maneuvers and set pieces before they have the skill to execute them adequately. The great players will choose an option requiring a simple task before "getting fancy," because they know they can execute it correctly and consistently. If a player cannot perform tasks properly, or with reasonable success, time should be spent on basic technical review. Working in groups of two to four on isolated maneuvers and set pieces, adjusted to player capabilities, will achieve the necessary consistency.

After a technique has been practiced under increasing pressure, with increasing accuracy and speed, it should be put to the test in a game. The performance should be reviewed after the game to ascertain reasons for any failures. In this way strengths and weaknesses can be determined and decisions made on how to correct any shortcomings.

The purpose of this section, then, is to provide drills that can be adapted according to the needs and desires of players and coaches. Consider one drill that can be used to build skill under pressure: a simple 2 v 1 (two versus one) keep-away game inside a grid with an unlimited number of touches allowed. When the two players can consistently keep the ball away from the one, they have learned to play it correctly. When the players can play the game well, the space is decreased and/or the number of touches allowed is decreased.

Suddenly this simple drill is not so easy anymore. It is important, therefore, to limit the space and the time available in order to increase the speed of execution, and to constantly challenge players in order to maintain skill level.

When we need confined spaces to work on developing skill, we use the *grid*. A grid is a number of equal-size squares in each of which a limited number of players can participate. This size of square varies with the objective. An area with few players allows more space and time, thus requiring less skill. More skill is required in a confined area with more players and less space and time.

Figure 4.1 shows a permanent grid and some simple drills:

1 v 1 with two resting partners taking turns
2 v 2, confined to two squares and with two small games
2 v 1 keep-away, 3 v 1 keep-away, and 3 v 3 game with two small goals

In the absence of facilities for a permanent grid, a temporary grid may be marked off with cones.

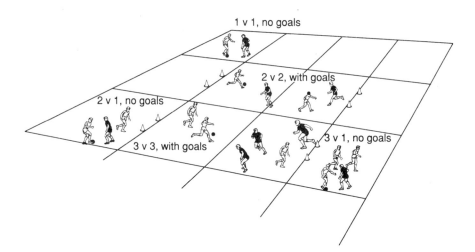

Figure 4.1
A permanent grid and some simple drills.

How to Make a Drill

Most coaches are constantly seeking new drills for practice. Many coaches invent their own drills to sharpen skills, teach set pieces, or implement tactical moves. When setting up a drill, the following principles are important.

1. Define your need.
2. Consider the players' age and technical level.
3. Make the drill as game-like as possible.
4. Do not waste time in unnecessary explanation; make corrections as the drill is executed.
5. If the drill is difficult or complicated, have the players walk through it first.
6. Keep the players active; allow for a ratio of no more than two minutes rest to one minute of work.
7. The drill should have faster than game rhythm.
8. The drill shouldn't cause injury to the players.
9. Tell the players what parts of the drill may not be game-like, so they will not repeat those parts in a game.

A Sample Drill

Coaches should build a repertoire of drills for most types of practices and make players aware of what they are doing and the intended goal. Here is an example:

Problem: The defense is having difficulty in getting rid of the ball in the penalty area. The players need to get used to meeting and controlling the ball, or just getting it away from this area. The players are not very skilled; they are 15 years old.

1. Divide the squad into groups of three.
2. For each group, place two players (A and B) 30 yards apart and the other (C) is in the middle.
3. Use two balls.
4. Player A passes a fast ball to C's right side. C meets it and in two touches (controlling the ball, then kicking it) passes back to A. B immediately passes to C's left side, and C, allowed two touches, passes back to B. If this is too difficult, allow C more touches. As C gets used to returning the ball, increase the frequency of passes from A and B to pressure C. If C seems to respond well, allow fewer touches.

As skill improves, the frequency of passes is increased and the time for control is thus decreased. Depending upon the player's condition, alternate C after receiving ten passes with A and then with B. (See Figure 4.2.)

Once the players are accustomed to the drill, continue it in front of a goal. Place 2 players 15 yards in front of the goal; place 7-10 players 20-40 yards away from the penalty area. The 7-10 players each have a ball and send hard passes, low or high, in sequence and at a rapid pace, aimed at the two players in the goal-area. The receivers must decide which person should clear which ball. As the drill progresses, the frequency and intensity of the moving balls become

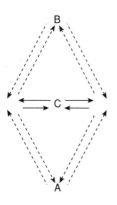

Figure 4.2
Players A and B alternate in passing wide of C.

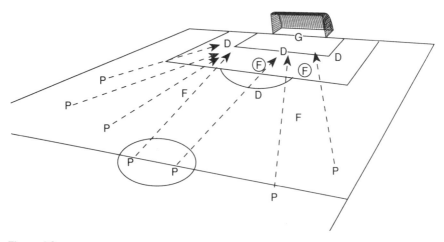

Figure 4.3
A number of passers (P) send long passes intended to land in the penalty area for two forwards (F), who are backed up by another two forwards. Four defenders (D) are also used.

more game-like. After 10–15 balls each (or 30 balls), the players in the goal area change places with 2 players from the kicking area.

To continue further, introduce a goalie and send the balls so that all three in the goal area must decide which one will get which ball. Now they have to learn to intercept and release the ball while the free player or players assume the position of backup. This drill can be modified to include balls coming from both sides of the goal, as with cross passes in a game. Here goalies and defenders must learn to intercept, time their jumps, and know without hesitation who will be the receiver and who will be the backup (be careful to avoid collisions).

To make the drill even more game-like, add a couple of forwards to accustom these forwards to heading or shooting under pressure. Add some backup players for the forwards so that if the ball is repelled in front of the penalty area, a shot may be taken or a pass made for a support player to shoot. Then add a defender in front of the penalty area to intercept any dangerous deflections and to prevent the backup forwards from intercepting the ball. (See Figure 4.3.)

This example shows how to start with a basic three-player drill and build it up to a whole team drill as the difficulty is increased. The same drill can be adapted for 8- to 10-year-olds by using ground balls only, from shorter distances, with one or two receivers in front of the goal area.

The frequency of the passes made should be determined by the players' level of competence. Make it competitive by saying something like, "Let's see how many balls we can kick away from the goal," or "Let's see how far we can kick them." Younger players rarely head or lift the ball and do not yet have the power for long passes or crosses, so do not expect perfect crosses or "clears" (kicking the ball away from the goal area). The coach should have patience until the players become familiar with the drill, then make changes to improve their performance.

Conditioning

In order to prevent muscle injury, a period of 10–15 minutes of warmup and stretching is necessary before practice begins. Stretching should not commence before the muscles are warmed up by jogging around the field for about 10 minutes. This increases the blood flow to the muscle fibers, making them more pliable. *Important note:* The stretched muscle groups should be completely RELAXED. If the muscles are stretched before a gentle warmup, muscle fibers will develop microscopic tears, which heal as scar tissue. This scar tissue is not flexible, so sooner or later the scar tissue buildup will cause muscle strain and limit the range of motion.

Conditioning can be accomplished in several ways:

1. Increase the tempo (rhythm) of practice drills (avoid over resting between drills).
2. Play small-sided games, such as 3 v 3 or 4 v 4, etc. (for 10–15 minutes each).
3. Maintenance running, 3 to 7 miles (depending on the age of the players). The ultimate objective is to run approximately two consecutive 6-minute miles, or better if possible. (Cooper run, 16- to 18-year-olds.)
4. Thirty consecutive sprints of 25 yards each, between a jog and a walk (jog-sprint-walk), depending on the age and physical capabilities of the players.
5. End conditioning with calisthenics for leg, abdomen, and back muscles. Do up to 35 sit-ups: knees bent and heels on the ground, hands behind the head, elbows to touch knees (each sit-up); back curls: lie flat on the stomach, lift legs and upper body off the ground; push-ups: lie flat, face down, body straight, push up to arms length.

Basic Conditioning

The maximum level of conditioning needed at the top level of play in soccer would be equivalent to 5 to 7, 6½-minute miles.

This type of *aerobic* capacity should be geared for various ages and competitive levels.

For 12-year-olds, three miles of jogging without keeping time, three times a week, should be a good start.

The prospects walk and jog for three miles. Walk only when tired of jogging to "catch" one's breath.

This sequence is repeated as necessary. If the next day there is no muscle pain, repeat the run at a faster pace to challenge one's body endurance and build stamina. When pain sets in the next day allow for rest.

For all ages the *time* and *distance* must be adjusted, reaching the maximum at age 19.

Performance per unit time must be considered as players mature. This develops a desirable *game rhythm*. First observed in practice it must become habitually high so it can carry and be an asset in the game.

Running is time-consuming and if at all possible should take place separately from regular practice. Conditioning is a personal discipline needed for optimum performance.

Practice time should be centered around skill, tactics, and small-sided games, learning to play together and maintaining high intensity level. If this carries in the game we have been successful.

Warmups

Players can warm up by running slowly for 10 minutes without the ball, or they can work with the ball, dribbling slowly in various directions, passing the ball gently back and forth, juggling while moving, practicing fakes, feints, dribbling moves, or in any other form of exercise that warms the muscles up gradually. Once warmed up, the players should stretch the main groups of muscles, as illustrated in Figure 4.4a–g.

Figure 4.4a
Stretching basic muscle groups. Right leg crossed over left, then left leg crossed over right (bend and hold each position 10–15 seconds). With knees straight and toes squared, bend and hold 10–15 seconds.

Figure 4.4b
Hold toe to stretch the front of the thigh. Alternate legs.

c

d

e

Figure 4.4c–e
c–d) Stretch calf, with feet wide and hands on front knee and the heel on the ground. The right toe should be pointed toward left heel. Alternate legs. e) The stretch is similar to the previous one, but now the back knee is bent and front knee is straight. Again, alternate legs.

Figure 4.4f
With legs spread wide and left foot in front, lean forward on left knee. The right toe should face front, with left toe perpendicular. Alternate legs. Same as previous stretch, except the left knee is bent and the trunk pushes down. Use hands to push upper body straight to vertical position. Alternate position of legs.

Figure 4.4g
Similar to the first stretch in f, but push on buttocks and bend back upper body.

Hamstrings (see Figure 4.4a)

Semitendinosus (hamstrings) are the muscles in the backs of the thighs. Stretch these by touching the toes with the fingers while keeping the knees straight. To facilitate this, put one leg in front of the other. The front leg forces the back leg's knee to stay straight. Hold it for 10–15 seconds, then reverse the position to stretch the other leg for the same amount of time. Then place the feet together, side by side, and with the knees straight touch the toes with the fingers.

Quadriceps (see Figure 4.4b)

This is the large muscle in the front of the thigh. Stand up, lift the right foot up to the buttocks, grab the toe stretched with the right hand, and point the knee toward the ground. Hold for 10 seconds then switch legs.

Gastrocnemius, Soleus, and Achilles Tendon of the Lower Leg (see Figure 4.4c,d,e)

The gastrocnemius is one of the calf muscles. Stretch it by taking a step forward so the feet are 3–4 feet apart and facing forward, as in a walking position. Bend the front knee while keeping the back knee straight and the back heel on the ground.

Now straighten the front knee and bend the back knee, keeping the back heel still on the ground. This stretches the soleus—the muscle underneath the calf muscle that attaches to the Achilles tendon—and the Achilles tendon as well. Switch legs and hold each of these positions for 10–15 seconds.

Groin (see Figure 4.4f,g)

Spread the legs 4–5 feet apart, facing forward and standing up. The right toe points forward with the left toe pointing outside at a 90-degree angle from the direction of the right foot. Bend the left knee way down. The body forms a diagonal line with the right leg and thigh. Rest both hands on the left knee and hold for 10–15 seconds. Push back with the hands on the left knee and straighten the upper body so it is in a vertical position. Hold for 10–15 seconds and then switch legs.

After stretching both legs, keep the legs spread apart. Make two fists and put the knuckles on the upper part of the buttocks and push the midsection of the body forward. Bend the body backward as much as possible and hold for 10–15 seconds.

All these exercises are designed to keep players off the ground when it is cold or wet. They are basic exercises that stretch the major muscle groups in the lower part of the body. There are many more stances designed to accomplish the same goal. The important thing is to relax the group of muscles to be stretched.

If a position is painful or extremely uncomfortable, the player should stop the exercise; this indicates overstretching, which will tear muscle tissues. Players should not bounce up and down to force the stretching; this method, called "ballistic stretching," tears the fibers. A normal stretch is held for 10–15 seconds, depending on the stiffness of the individual.

Remember, too, that the player is cooling down while stretching, so after stretching he or she should warm up again for about 5 minutes.

Alternatively, players may warm up for 5 minutes, stretch only one group of muscles, warm up some more, stretch another group, and so on until the major muscle groups are adequately stretched. In either case, warming up and stretching for 20–30 minutes is desirable and strongly recommended. If weather is poor, try to warm up and stretch indoors and then go out and train.

Remember, stretching cannot prevent pulled muscles if the player does not maintain a constant game rhythm during practice, i.e., players should keep jogging in place when standing in line for a drill. Muscle injury is possible even *with* proper warmups and stretching; however, if the player is prepared and maintains game rhythm, the probability is slight. Constant practice rhythm becomes habitual and carries over into games.

A Word on Vision

Our world emphasizes looking and focusing our vision on people and objects, either to remember details or because it is customary. We must learn to consciously pay attention to our full field of vision—which means using the visual abilities that our anatomy gives us.

We are endowed with 180 degrees of *lateral* vision. *Vertically,* eyebrows and cheekbones partially reduce the range of vision, because they protrude from the face. By tilting the head forward 15 percent, we should be able to distinguish the ball at our feet while looking 10–30 yards away.

With peripheral vision, the ability to distinguish colors fades progressively with distance to the side. However, it is unnecessary to look directly at an opponent or the ball, since colors and details have no bearing on the ability to control and distribute the ball.

In a 20- by 20-yard area, with players evenly spread out along the sidelines, if we look at the ground somewhere in the middle we should be able to see everyone. By distinguishing the uniforms' limited shades, we can pick up the spaces available and the players' movements. This new awareness, properly developed, will eventually become a part of the subconscious and cause intuitive reactions. Eventually the field of vision will encompass most of the playing area, immensely enlarging the understanding of the game. The drills presented below are designed to develop peripheral vision.

1. Players jog in line, 10 feet apart. Each player tilts his or her head forward slightly and looks at the heels of the player in front while dribbling a ball, keeping the ball close to his or her feet.
2. Free dribbling with the ball, looking ahead 6–10 feet but not focusing on anything in particular. Keep the ball very close to the feet. Be aware of movement, the location of others, and the spaces available. (See Figure 4.5.)
3. All players dribble in a confined area, 15- by 15-yards, slowly at first and then faster. Players look ahead of the ball and run to open areas in order to avoid running into each other.

Figure 4.5
The players look ahead, move to open spaces, and keep the balls close to their feet.

4. Players are positioned ten yards apart, facing one another. A single marker is placed eight feet to the front and three feet to the side of each player. The players focus on the markers, with their heads bent slightly forward, while passing a ball back and forth.
5. A marker is placed at the center of a 15-yard square. Four players are positioned at the corners of the square and are instructed to focus on the marker while passing the ball around the perimeter of the square. (See Figure 4.6.)
6. Four players are placed at the corners of a 15-yard square, given two balls, and instructed to pass to free players, making sure no player receives two balls at a time. Their eyes should be focused on the center of the square so that all other players remain within the field of peripheral vision. (See Figure 4.7.)
7. Three players are positioned at the corners of a square and given two balls. Player 1 passes the ball to the open corner and runs to the corner vacated by 2. 2 runs to the open corner to intercept 1's pass. 3 passes the ball to the corner vacated by 2, where it will be intercepted by 1. Repeat the cycle, modified for the new position of the open corner. (See Figure 4.8.)

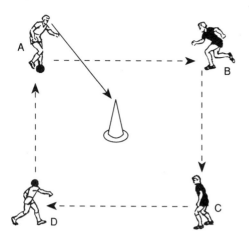

Figure 4.6
The players focus on the marker while passing the ball around the perimeter, from player A to B, to C, etc.

Figure 4.7
Several squares are marked off with cones. In the foreground, note the player on the right preparing to pass to the far left (center cone in foreground) while the middle player is moving to intercept the ball.

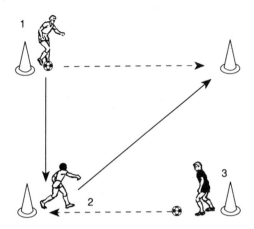

Figure 4.8
Player 1 passes to the free marker, then runs to the area vacated by player 2, who has gone to intercept the pass. Meanwhile player 3 sends a ball to the area vacated by 2, which will be intercepted by 1.

What Position Should I Play?

5

Since the development of systems, members of a team have received various names, according to the duties they perform.

The *goalie* protects the goal and can use his or her hands in the penalty area (44 yards wide and 18 yards long) on the defensive end of the field.

The *backs* are divided into *fullbacks,* who usually protect the area in front of the goal from touchline to touchline, and *halfbacks,* who play immediately in front of the fullbacks from touchline to touchline.

The *forwards* are divided into *wings,* who play wide on either side and up and down the length of the field, and *inside forwards,* who play on each side of the field, helping the wings and linking them with the halfbacks and the *center forward,* who plays in the center area of the defending team's side of the field. Because of this positioning, the center forward is intended to be the team's main scorer.

As systems changed and new ones emerged, positional nomenclature was altered accordingly. The outside defenders playing close to the edge of the field became the *wing backs* or *outside backs* (or just plain right and left backs). The central defender, who mostly "marks" (covers one-on-one) the center forward, was called a *stopper;* the other defender, who roams in back of the other three and does not mark a player, was a *sweeper.* A sweeper whose duty includes moving upfield and helping the halfbacks or the forwards is called a *libero.*

The halfbacks and inside forwards became *midfielders.* These positions were in turn divided into right, left, attacking, and defending midfielders according to the roles assigned them.

The wing forwards and center forward did not change much. At times, when two center forwards are used, one becomes an *attacking center forward* and the other a *backup center forward.* Sometimes the attacking center forward will become a "target" player for long upfield passes. The target player's job is to control the ball and pass, or play the ball first time (with one touch) to supporting teammates. Thus, the target player can set up other teammates, or himself or herself, for a cross or shots on goal.

The names of positions will continue to evolve with the game. Now that each player's position is generally understood, we can investigate the basic qualities demanded of the various positions.

The Goalie

Besides a good pair of steady strong hands, the goalie should have:

- An excellent vertical leap so that the hands of the goalie are able to reach a ball 10 or more féet in the air and *still hold on to it.*
- Good anticipation of where an opponent will shoot or cross the ball.
- Patience and composure to know when to come off the goal line and catch a cross or to win a one-on-one (when an attacking player is isolated against a defending player, in this case the goalie, and tries to beat him).
- Courage to face a dangerous situation, such as a one-on-one, or to make a diving catch among a number of players.

The goalie is a specialist, the only player allowed to use his or her hands throughout the game. For this reason, the goalie should have separate training sessions to practice specialized techniques. The goalie should be involved with the team whenever there is a shooting drill or exercise that involves the goalie in a tactical situation.

I recommend that all teams have two goalies; they can train together and back each other up in practice. Also, if one is injured, there will be a backup for games.

Basic Goalie Exercises

1. Standing 2 to 3 yards away, roll or kick a ground ball at medium speed 3 to 4 steps to the goalie's right or left so that the goalie must move to pick up the ball. If he or she goes to the left (or right), while picking up the ball, the right (left) knee should drop to the ground about 6 inches from the heel of the left (right) foot (see Figure 5.1). If the ball goes through the goalie's hands, this technique prevents the ball from going through the legs and into the goal. Once the ball is secured in the hands, it should be curled up into the chest. Alternate kicking and throwing balls to the right and left for about 30 repetitions.
2. This time the goalie should be in a sitting position with feet out in front and spread wide (see Figure 5.2). Again, from 2 or 3 yards away, the ball is thrown or kicked *as far as the goalie can reach:* center, midcenter, and off-center, to the right and to the left. As the goalie catches it, the ball is clutched to the chest to break the goalie's fall. Continue for 5 sets of 6 repetitions.
3. This exercise is the same as number 2, except that the goalie starts on his or her knees. It should also be done for 5 sets of 6 repetitions. (See Figure 5.3.)
4. Place a marker (a cone or pylon will do) on the ground. Pick an area that is not too hard. Have the goalie touch the marker with the left hand as you throw a ball gently to his or her right, far enough that he or she must dive in order to catch it. Be sure that the goalie dives on his or her side, as practiced in the first three drills, pulling ball and knees to the chest as the body

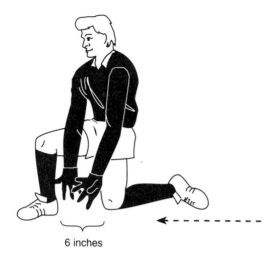

6 inches

Figure 5.1
As a goalie picks up the ball, the back knee is parallel to the ground while the front knee is approximately at a 90° angle. Both hands are in front of the back knee to catch the ball. The move is actually *sideways* (like a shortstop in baseball).

Figure 5.2
While in the sitting position, the goalie fields 5 gentle passes, directed for maximum reach, for a total of 35 passes.

Figure 5.3
While kneeling, but not sitting on his heels, the goalie fields and returns a total of 35 balls directed to make him or her reach.

Figure 5.4
The goalie touches a marker before diving to the right or left to catch the ball.

hits the ground so that he or she can roll, if necessary. Start with easy ground balls, then go higher as the goalie becomes more adept at falling. This should be done in two sets of 15, one set right and one set left. (See Figure 5.4.)

5. Place two goalies 30 to 40 yards apart and have them throw balls to each other with a straight one-hand overarm throw. (Adjust the distance for younger players.) As the ball is thrown high, it must be caught by the other goalie at the highest point at which he or she can jump and catch it with arms extended. Catching it, he or she curls it into the chest with both hands. When the ball is being caught, both hands must be in a bowl-like shape so that if the thumbs are touching, the two index fingers form a "W." The rest of the fingers are partially spread so they can cover a greater surface area of the ball for greater control.

When jumping for the ball, the goalie should jump off one foot and bring the opposite knee up to the chest so that the back of the uplifted foot is parallel to the ground (see Figure 5.5). This allows the goalie maximum height for the jump while providing protection against an opposing player who charges into him or her during game conditions. This should be done for 30–40 repetitions.

6. Throw the goalie high balls (as high as can be reached) and slightly in front (short) to get him or her used to coming out and catching the ball at the highest point possible. The balls should be thrown from the right and left side of the goal, as a cross toward the center would be made in a game by an upcoming forward (30 repetitions per side). Catching the ball at the highest point decreases the possibility of an opposing player heading the ball into the goal.

7. Place 6 cones, 14 inches high, in front of the goal, 2 feet apart from each other and on a parallel line 10 feet out from the goal line. The idea is to shoot the ball low so that some of the shots will deflect off the cones, forcing the goalie to improve anticipation and reaction to the flight of the ball.

Figure 5.5
Lifting one knee allows the goalie to jump higher.

8. Place a marker in the center of the goal. The goalie comes out and attempts to intercept an incoming forward. The forward, starting from about 30 yards out, moves very fast toward the goalie and tries to *place* a soft shot by him. As the play is ended, the goalie recovers by going back to touch the marker before coming out again to meet the next attacker. As the goalie improves, increase the number of repetitions (5 at a time). Alternate goalies and have the forwards come at the goalie every 4 seconds. Continue for 6 sets of 5 repetitions. This is a strenuous drill, and it is important to allow the goalie adequate time to rest between sets.
9. Players approach from 40 yards out and shoot from the 18-yard line. The goalie stays on the goal line and stops as many shots as possible. The frequency is 4 seconds between incoming players. Alternate goalies after five shots. Each goalie tries 6 sets of 5 repetitions.
10. Two lines of players in a column approach from 40 yards out. The players shoot from 20 yards out. Each line sends players independently of the other, every 4 seconds. The goalie tries to stop both shots. Since the average frequency between shots is about 2 seconds, he or she should be able to save 1 shot and block the other or recover as quickly as possible.
11. The goalies stand far apart and practice kicking long balls to each other. Each should take 30 punts, 30 drop kicks, and 30 goal kicks.

Goalkeeper Kicking

When punting or drop-kicking the ball, do not throw the ball up in the air; rather, hold the ball low and drop it onto the foot. This decreases the probability of striking the ball off-center and thus spinning it off the foot and away from the intended target. The power and distance of the kick come from the swing of the foot by the knee. The thigh acts as a whip handle, which sets the whip in motion, and the knee is the pivot point that allows the foot to pick up speed for the whip. (This is true of all kicks that are struck from the instep of the foot.)

The technique for drop-kicking is the same, with the exception of timing. In this case, the ball is dropped to the ground and struck the moment it rebounds. It must be no more than an inch above the ground when it is hit. If the timing is late, the ball will go straight up; if it is too early, it will be a line drive along the ground. A successful drop kick will travel much farther than a punt and will require less effort.

Drop kicks are more desirable because, in addition to traveling farther, they fly lower to the ground than punts, reaching the intended target earlier, making it difficult for opposing defenders to stop and easier for forwards to get to and control. However, they are difficult to master and kick consistently well, particularly in bad weather or on a poor field surface.

For a goal kick, the ball is placed on the ground. The goalie should approach the ball from a 45-degree angle. The instep of the foot should strike the ball below its center point. The nonkicking foot should be about one foot diagonally behind of the ball.

Goalie Agility Drills (adjust for age)

1. The goalie places the ball on the ground, jumps sideways over the ball, landing on the other foot. Continue jumping side to side for 20 repetitions.
2. The goalie places the ball on the ground, then jumps forward over the ball, landing on the opposite foot. He or she then jumps backwards, landing on the other foot. Continue back and forth for 20 repetitions.
3. Same as number 1 except both feet are kept together.
4. Same as number 2 except both feet are kept together.
5. Combination of numbers 1 and 2, jumping right to left then front and back, for 10 full repetitions.
6. The goalie lies on the ground face down, throws the ball high up in the air with both hands, gets up, catches it, and brings it to the chest. The same exercise can be done with a partner throwing the ball up in the air: using two balls, throw one up, let the goalie catch it and put it down. When the goalie lies back down, throw the other ball up in the air 5 to 10 yards away. As he or she goes to catch that ball, pick the other one up and throw it 5 to 10 yards away. (One set of five repetitions for each variation.)

   Be sure the goalie concentrates on:

   • jumping off one foot and bringing the other knee up to the chest (this helps increase the height of the jump);
   • meeting and catching the ball at the highest point possible;
   • bringing the ball into the chest;
   • landing on the same (the jumping) foot.
7. The same as number 6 except the goalie begins on the ground face up.

Figure 5.6
Kick to a partner 25 yards away using two touches: one touch to trap and prepare the ball for the second touch, the second touch to drive the ball back to the partner.

The Outside Fullbacks

The *wing fullback* or *outside fullback* should have good speed and stamina for long overlapping runs (where the fullback carries or runs to meet the ball upfield, beyond the midfielders, thus "overlapping" them); toughness in tackling the ball; and quickness in turning to recover against an attacker. The outside back must be able to stop an opponent from penetrating the defense. In corner kicks, he or she should be able to deflect incoming balls and win them from an opponent in the air or on the ground. On the attack, this player should be able to beat an opponent with the dribble.

Drills for Outside Fullbacks

1. Kick to a partner 25 yards away using two touches: one touch to trap and prepare the ball for the second touch, the second touch driving the ball back to the partner. (See Figure 5.6.)
2. After 10 minutes of the drill above, move 40 yards apart and continue for another 10 minutes. Use only one touch to drive the ball accurately back to the partner.
3. One-on-one, shielding the ball for 1 to 2 minutes. (To "shield" the ball means to keep your body between the ball and the opponent.) (See Figure 5.7.)

Figure 5.7
Shielding the ball from a defender.

4. One-on-one, jockeying an opponent up and down the field for 1 to 2 minutes. (See Figure 5.8.)
5. 2 v 1 keep-away in a small area (ten yards square).
6. Player A passes a *short* ball to player B, who comes to meet the ball. Player C follows closely and does not allow B to turn with the ball without losing it.
7. Rehearse one or two fakes against an opponent.

The Stopper (Centerback)

Stoppers are usually very strong on the ball, specifically in defensive tackling, and very strong on winning air balls. They must anticipate readily what an attacking forward intends to do with the ball. They should be able to hinder an attacking forward from receiving and controlling the ball, or prevent the attacking forward who does gain control of the ball from turning with it. They should be able to recognize attempts by an attacking forward to draw them out of position.

When the stopper is pulled out, someone else should cover the position (normally the sweeper), since the middle of the defensive third (i.e., the defensive third of the field) is the most effective spot to attack the goal. This is why the centerback (or stopper) should be very capable in repelling attacks. Like the outside backs, the stopper should be able to initiate the attack.

Figure 5.8
Jockeying an opponent with the ball.

Drills for Stoppers

1. 2 v 2 to goal with *tight* marking. Have a free third player pass to the moving targets.
2. Same as number 1, but 3 v 3 or 4 v 4, with another player making passes to the moving targets.
3. Two defenders stand in front of the goal. Five to seven players serve lofted balls, from 40 to 50 yards out. Each must be cleared first time (i.e., with one touch) away from the goal. A clear should at least pass outside the penalty box (otherwise, in a game, an attacking player would shoot the ball right back at the goal). To simulate a game situation, a player may roam about the edge of the penalty box and shoot, first time, any balls that do not clear the box. The serving players should make their passes every 4 seconds. (See Figure 5.9.)

The Sweeper and the Libero

These terms refer to the player behind the fullbacks who does not usually mark a particular player. Most modern teams use one; some occasionally use two. This player's job is to back up the fullbacks and the stopper and prevent any breakdown in the defense. When playing in back of the fullbacks, he or she is a true

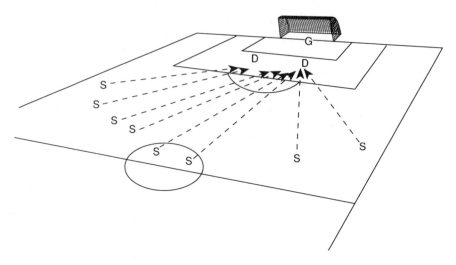

Figure 5.9
Servers (S) pass balls into the penalty area, to be cleared by two defenders (D) with one touch.

sweeper. In certain situations, on the other hand, a *libero* may move in front of this last defensive line or even further, assisting in midfield play and even scoring goals.

The libero is as versatile as the midfielders but is also a superior defender. He or she must have great mobility skill. In skill and understanding of the game, as well as physical attributes, liberos are often superior to most of their teammates. Many can play this position, but the real outstanding ones are rare.

Drills for Sweepers and Liberos

1. Attacker A moves with the ball toward the goal from 40 yards out. Defender B jockeys A. Defender C arrives and tackles the ball from A. If C misses and A still has the ball, B tackles A, and so on until they win the ball or A scores. (Player B must jockey only on the right or the left of the attacker in order for C to know where to come for the tackle. This drill is appropriate for fullbacks, too.)
2. 3 v 3 with the libero in the middle playing on whichever side has the ball. When team A or B attacks, the libero backs them up. (See Figure 5.10.)
3. Four perimeter players send 40-yard fast balls to players A and B; they then pass back to the sweeper/libero, who sends the ball back to one of the perimeter players who has called for the ball. (See Figure 5.11.)

The Midfielders

The midfielders, who are usually the playmakers of the team, must have outstanding ball control, tackle hard defensively, hold the ball until a receiver is

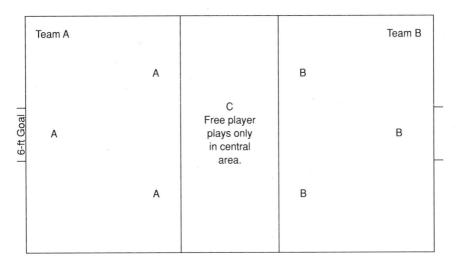

Figure 5.10
A 3 v 3 game played on the whole field. The free fourth player is restricted to the central area.

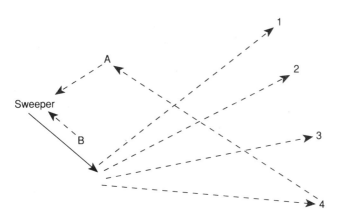

Figure 5.11
A drill utilizing the sweeper/libero.

positioned properly (if necessary), and time their passes to lead receivers into available space. They should be good dribblers and have a superior knowledge of game tactics. The midfielder must know when a ball should be passed to another player's feet or lead a player into space.

The midfielder is soccer's equivalent of a quarterback in football, so the more creativity, the better. Size is not a great factor, but usually midfielders are of average size, quick, and able to run for hours on end, because they go wherever they are needed on the field, from goal to goal, helping both the defense and the attack.

To divide the work load, midfielders are designated right, left, attacking, or defending. They switch roles as necessary and share both the defensive and offensive chores.

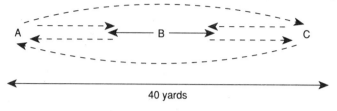

Figure 5.12
A makes a short pass to B, who runs to meet the ball. B passes back to A, who makes a high, long pass to C while B runs back to intercept.

Drills for Midfielders

1. Players A and C stand 40 yards apart. Player B runs to meet a short pass from A and passes back to A, who makes a high pass to C. B turns, runs, and receives the ball from C and passes it back. Players exchange roles until each has had 15 repetitions. (See Figure 5.12.)
2. Same as number 1 except B meets the pass from A, turns, and passes to C; then C passes back to B, who meets it, turns, and passes to A, etc.
3. A passes to B from 20 yards. B runs, meets the ball, and passes it back while under pressure from C. A receives the ball and chips the ball away *for C to intercept* and B to apply pressure, etc. (Repeat 10 times before switching player positions.)
4. A coach passes the ball to player A, who comes to meet it, turns, and passes to a called-out target, B, C, D, or E. Repeat 10 times, after which the players alternate (work both feet). (See Figure 5.13.)

The Forwards (Wings and Center Forwards)

The forward must be fast and quick *or* very strong at shielding and keeping possession of the ball in front of the goal or penalty area. The forward makes an ideal target player. The player should be an outstanding dribbler and be able to shoot on goal from a first-time touch.

Fast forwards are hard to stop or even slow down with only one defender, which increases their value. A fast forward either keeps two defenders busy or is likely to break loose and score. A superior target player is also a great asset because he or she is able to control the ball and set up teammates in dangerous areas in front of the goal while drawing more than one defender.

The forward should be able to shoot equally well with either foot, since time is limited in the attacking third of the field and there is usually less space and time for a pass or shot.

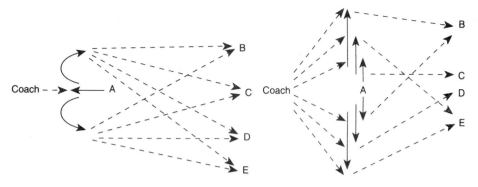

Figure 5.13
Left) A coach passes the ball to player A, who comes to meet it, turns, and passes to a called-out target, B, C, D, or E. Repeat ten times, after which the players alternate. Try both sides (left foot, right foot). Right) Same as left except player A shoots the first time.

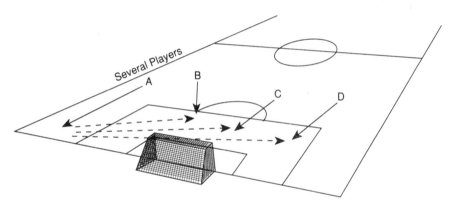

Figure 5.14
Player A brings the ball down the touchline and makes centering passes for teammates B, C, and D.

Drills for Forwards

1. A player takes the ball down the touchline and then centers it to teammates who are running to the near post, the far post, and the penalty spot. The teammates shoot the ball into the goal. Work for accuracy of the cross, timing of the runs, and accuracy of the shot. (See Figure 5.14.)
2. Same as number 1, except the ball is crossed to the far post from about 15 yards out. The far-post player plays the ball first time or controls it and then crosses it to the players on line with the other post for a shot. The purpose is to get players to think about setting up other teammates if they themselves do not have a good opportunity to score.
3. Same as drills 1 and 2, except the receiver *heads* the ball at the goal or to a teammate for a shot. This is to work on the timing of heading the ball and to develop a good head shot.

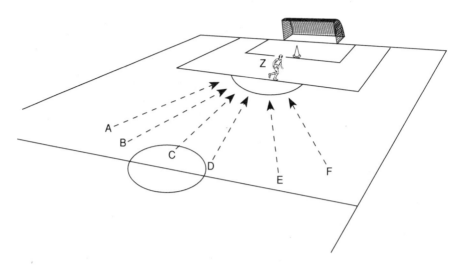

Figure 5.15
Players A through F, in order, send high, long balls to player Z. See #4 below for explanation.

4. Players A–F, in order, send high, long balls to player Z. (See Figure 5.15.)
Z *runs* from the cone and meets the ball, turns with it, and shoots on goal.
Z should turn the ball with the first touch and shoot the ball with the second.
After shooting, Z runs back and touches the cone on the 6-yard line and turns
to receive the next ball in flight. A ball should be sent every 6 to 7 seconds,
for 5 to 10 repetitions. Then rotate the perimeter players one by one into the
Z position until everyone has had a turn as Z.
5. The coach (or a number of teammates) serves lead passes to player Z. Z chases
the ball and shoots on goal, then returns to the marker before chasing the next
ball. The shot should be taken first time. If the pass is too short, Z should touch
it one time and push it about 3 yards ahead to prepare for the second touch,
which should be a shot. Balls are passed in rapid succession for 5 to 10 repetitions. The marker should be placed 30 yards in front of the goal.
6. A player slaloms with the ball between cones that are 6 to 10 feet apart
(using 8 to 10 cones). Always use the inside of the outside foot when cutting
to either side. Upon reaching the last cone, the player returns to the start.
The distance between cones depends on the skill of the player—the less skilled,
the greater the distance.

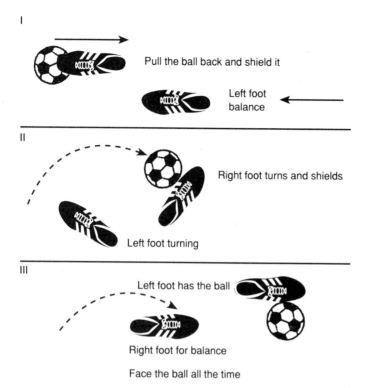

I

Pull the ball back and shield it

Left foot balance

II

Right foot turns and shields

Left foot turning

III

Left foot has the ball

Right foot for balance

Face the ball all the time

Figure 5.16
See above.

7. The player dribbles the ball and suddenly cuts (changing the direction of the ball, at a 90-degree angle or less) when arriving at a cone. Learn to cut equally well with either foot.
8. The player dribbles the ball forward then pulls it back with the tip of the sole, while *shielding* it with the same foot. The ball is never in back of the pulling foot as the body pivots on the other foot. (See Figure 5.16.)

Individual Tactics

6

Dribbling

If there is no support player or receiver available, the ball carrier should look for an open space to dribble into. An effective dribble forces the defense to keep one or two defenders busy covering the player who is penetrating their defensive third. In a *one-on-one situation* and in your attacking third, dribble and try to pass the defender. If you are successful, another defender will have to release the player he or she is marking to cover you. Having drawn the second defender, you can now pass to a free teammate, who can advance toward the goal or draw the sweeper. As attackers and defenders are even in number any mistake can be costly for the defending team.

Fakes

A *fake* may be executed when receiving, passing, or dribbling the ball. It may be used to pull a defensive player out of position, thereby *giving a teammate more time* to shoot, execute a better pass, or draw another opponent out of position.

Superior results are achieved by those who have enough time to execute plays. Poor covering and/or poor positioning by the defense allows the offense more time to execute; inadequate movement off the ball by the offense allows the defense more time to organize; and poor conditioning or lack of concentration on the part of either team allows their opponents more time. When both sides are at the same technical and conditioning level, the successful team will be the one better able to utilize fakes.

Players who use good fakes create unpredictable situations. Their opponents never know what to expect, and this uncertainty puts great pressure on the opposition, both physically and psychologically. When one team is consistently deceived, it is thrown off-balance and must devote extra attention to stopping the opponent. This decreases their chance of mounting an attack. Since fakes are very flashy, they are also crowd-pleasers.

Continuous rehearsal of fakes should be mandatory for all levels and ages. Start with simple exercises, such as dribbling passively (without an opponent, like shadow-boxing) and rehearsing fakes. Players can also practice fakes and improve their dribbling skills in 1 v 1 and 2 v 1 games. They can learn and perfect

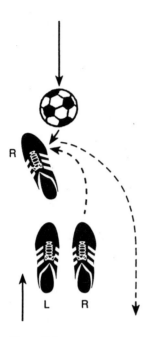

Figure 6.1a
Basic fakes. The over-the-foot fake. As the ball quickly approaches the left foot, the right foot meets the ball and directs it to the right side. This quick motion takes the opponent by surprise.

fakes by copying other players and then developing their own style. A player who knows only one fake has a 50-50 chance of beating a defender; once three moves are perfected, the probability increases to 75 percent. (See Figure 6.1a–c.)

Shielding the Ball

Shielding is a technique used to keep possession of the ball (see Figure 6.2). It can buy time for a player who has nowhere to pass or dribble and must wait until a receiver is available. A player pinned against the goal line or touchline can use it to force an opponent to kick the ball out, resulting in either a throw-in or a corner kick.

A player should receive a teammate's pass on the side opposite the defender so that the body acts as a shield, allowing control of the ball. This makes it difficult for the defender to see the ball and tackle it without committing a foul. Shielding is even more productive in the penalty area, where the defender will be more reluctant to incur a foul and give a penalty kick to the attacking team. This effectively neutralizes the defender on the back of the player shielding the ball and creates options for the shielding player, such as making a backpass for a teammate to shoot or spinning around the defender for a shot on goal.

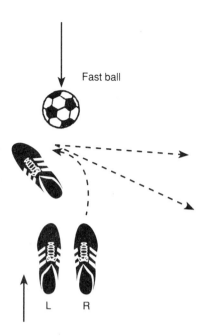

Fast ball

Figure 6.1b
The over-the-foot deflection pass. A quickly approaching ball may be deflected in several directions. The quick motion takes the opponent by surprise as to the direction of the pass.

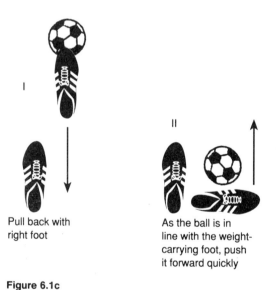

I

II

Pull back with
right foot

As the ball is in
line with the weight-
carrying foot, push
it forward quickly

Figure 6.1c
Pull back and push forward: the player with the ball moves forward, slows down, pulls the ball back slightly, then pushes it forward suddenly.

Figure 6.2
Shielding the ball.

The Dummy

When the intended receiver of a pass is drawing a defender and knows there is a teammate open to his or her side away from the passer, the intended receiver can let the pass go by as if he or she were a "dummy." This neutralizes the defender without slowing the game down, so the attacking team becomes one player up on a surprised defensive team, forcing them even further out of position. (See Figure 6.3a–b.)

Marking

Defensively, *marking* someone means playing at arm's length and staying *goalside,* that is, between the attacker and the goal. The distance from the player to be marked will vary in direct proportion to the proximity of the goal and the position of the ball—the closer the goal, the tighter the coverage. (See Figure 6.4.)

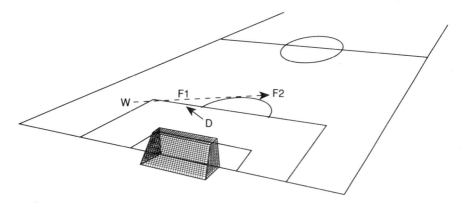

Figure 6.3a
The dummy. W sends a fast ground ball to F1, who is running in. D moves to intercept F1.
F1 steps over the ball, leaving it for F2.

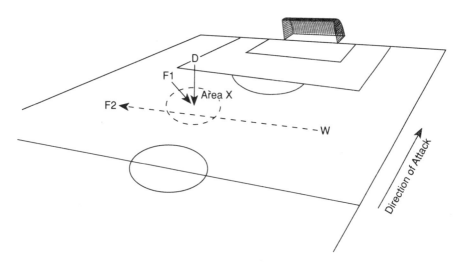

Figure 6.3b
W passes across the field to area X. F1 moves to receive the ball, drawing D, but steps over the
ball, leaving it for F2.

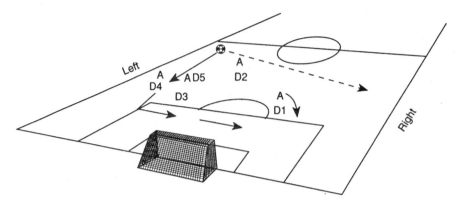

Figure 6.4
Marking the attackers (A). All defenders will move to cover if the forwards will shift.

Forcing the Play

A defensive player's object is to force the attacker to move in a predetermined direction, while denying the attacker his or her most effective route. In most instances, the attacker is forced away from the center of the field and away from the defending goal. However, if an attacker has difficulty in playing or shooting the ball with a particular foot, the defender should try to force that player to use the weak foot. By forcing the play, the defender can make the attacker do what the defender wants, making the attacker predictable and more apt to lose possession of the ball.

In Figure 6.5, defender D1 covers the inside of the field, forcing the attacker A to the outside. Knowing the inside is covered, D2 approaches to tackle on the opposite side. D1 then stops jockeying A and joins in the tackle.

Delaying

Defensively, delaying is done by jockeying the attacker to slow him or her down, giving the rest of the team time to get into a defensive position. Once they are in position, the defender should attempt to tackle the ball. If this doesn't work, there should be a backup player behind to cover the attacker.

Offensively, an attacker, if outnumbered after receiving the ball, should delay or slow the game down to give his or her teammates time to provide support. Once they are in position, the attacker should attempt to advance the ball.

Meeting the Ball

With few exceptions, the idea in soccer is always to *meet the ball unless you chase it.* The faster a player can meet the ball, the more time the player has to

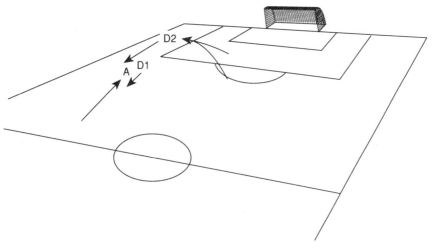

Figure 6.5
Forcing the play. D1 forces A on the outside while D2 comes to take on the attacker as D1 will
follow.

distribute it, turn with it, or do whatever the situation demands. Watching the
ball and waiting for it to arrive leads to loss of possession. An excellent drill for
this involves two players 40 yards apart and two players between, with one acting
as a defender. (See Figure 6.6.) The outside players pass to the player in the
middle, who moves to meet the ball. The defender may be passive (applying less
pressure) or active and attempt to intercept the ball and pass it back to the outside player. The successful receiver chips the ball to the other outside player, who

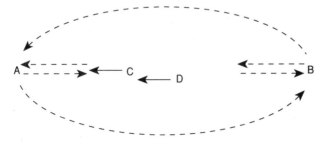

Figure 6.6
Meeting the ball: A passes to C, who runs to meet the ball, followed closely by defender D. C passes back to A, who chips the ball to B. Now D becomes the receiver and C the defender. In a variation, C must pass back and receive a later ball, beat D, and pass to B, who will now pass to D before the cycle is repeated.

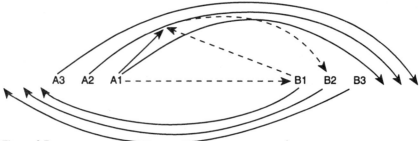

Figure 6.7
Meeting the ball: A1 passes to B1, then B1 passes wide to A1 and runs to the back of A3 while A1 goes to the back of B3 after he chips the ball to B2's head. B2 controls the ball and makes a ground pass to A2 (and goes to the back of A3), who makes a wide ground pass to B3. B3 chips the ball to A3 and so forth.

repeats the same procedure on the other side. The two middle players reverse roles each time the ball is chipped. A variation on this drill can be used to practice turning with the ball under pressure.

Another drill consists of two columns of players facing one another, 40 yards apart. The first player in column A, player A1, passes a ground ball to player B1, who controls the pass and returns the ball wide of column A. B1 then runs to the back of column A, while A1 moves to meet the ball and chips it to the head of B2 before running to the back of column B. Player B2 then renews the cycle by passing a ground ball to A2. (See Figure 6.7.)

See Figure 5.12 for another drill in meeting the ball.

Figure 6.8 offers a variation to the drill in Figure 6.6. In this case, A passes a low wide ball to C. C meets the pass and beats player D, then passes to B. C and D again reverse roles.

Turning with the Ball

Turning refers to a player who receives the ball while facing his or her own goal. Turning with the ball is not recommended unless the player is certain that no opponent is close enough to make a tackle. Since the player's back is turned from

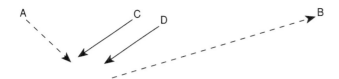

Figure 6.8
A passes a low, wide ball to C. C meets the pass and beats player D, then passes to B. C and D again reverse roles; while B makes a wide short pass to D, etc.

the intended direction of progress, this is hard to know for sure. Turning with the ball should only be attempted in the attacking third, where success puts the player in an ideal position to score and there is little chance of being scored on from a counterattack if possession is lost. However, turning is dangerous because an unexpected tackle can cause injury.

It is best for a player to pass back, turn *without* the ball, and present himself for a return pass. The player should move to meet the return pass and, having received it, proceed forward or cut on a 90-degree angle in case an opponent is just behind. In this instance, and in all cases of turning with or without the ball, the player must be aware of the possibility of being blindsided by an opponent unprepared for the move.

Technically, a turned player should always have a teammate in support to whom he or she can backpass. If there is no support, a quick glance behind while moving to meet the ball will tell if a turn is possible and in what direction.

From the defender's point of view, he or she must not allow the opponent to turn with the ball because the opponent becomes much more dangerous once he or she can see upfield. Further, the best time to steal the ball is when the opponent's back is turned. Because most players need time to control the ball before turning, the defender should "read" the pass and anticipate how the opponent will control it. This is the moment the defender should tackle. If the tackle doesn't succeed, the defender should delay in making a next move so that teammates can better predict what is coming.

The Outside Shot

When a forward shields the ball within the penalty area and elects not to turn with it, there should be a support player to whom he or she can give a backpass. Preferably, the ball should be passed back diagonally and anticipated by the teammate. At this point, unintentionally, the defenders often obstruct the goalie's view of the ball while covering the passer, so the receiver can concentrate on taking a good shot on goal. The outside shot is most effective from this type of back pass. For an attacker to dribble the ball and take the shot is much more predictable and easier for the goalie to see.

If the goalie's view is obstructed and if the outside shot is taken quickly, it is usually too late for the goalie to react. Further, the outside shot presents a dilemma to a defense that tends to back up and overcrowd their own defensive

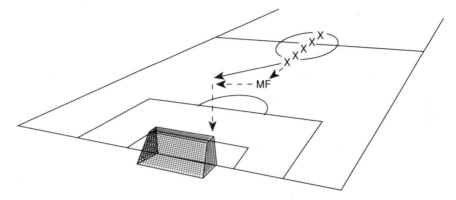

Figure 6.9
The first X player passes to MF and moves as indicated. MF gives a short lateral or diagonal pass to X, who shoots on goal.

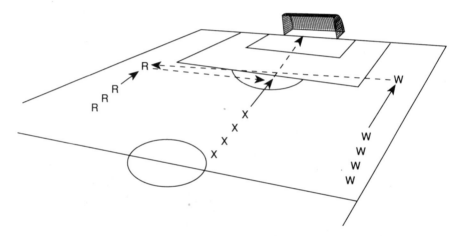

Figure 6.10
The first player W in line crosses the ball to the first R, who controls it and passes to the first X, who shoots on goal. Note how players are led by the pass, made to the space in front.

third. It is difficult to properly deflect or stop a hard, low outside shot; the deflected ball usually lands where another attacker can take an even better shot, since the defense cannot set up fast enough in the new location. Because a deflection is likely, offensive players should always be positioned and ready to follow up with a shot.

Good outside shooting forces the defense to come out and stop the shot, thus exposing themselves for a through ball (a ball passed between two defenders) or a chip into the space behind them. As the saying goes, "a good outside shot keeps the defense honest." For drill examples to improve outside shots, see Figures 6.9 through 6.12.

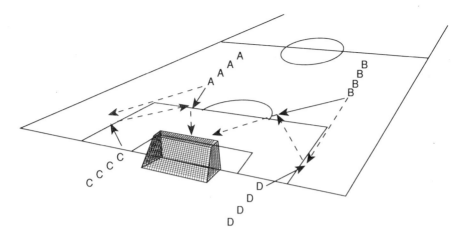

Figure 6.11
Players from lines A and B pass wide to C and D, respectively, who run to meet the ball. C and D set up A and B for shots on goal. After a shot, an A or B goes to the end of the C or D line and vice versa.

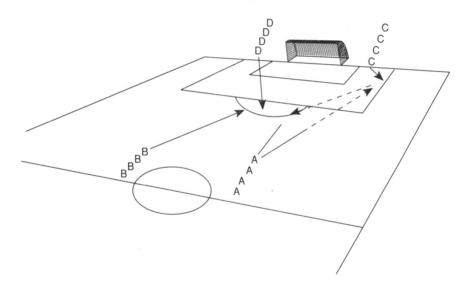

Figure 6.12
Players in column A dribble up and pass to column C players, who set up column A players while B players come up for support. Column D sends a defender so that there will be a 2 v 1 situation ending with a shot on goal.

The Chip Pass

Normally defenders can cover all possible ground angles but are almost defense-less against the short or long high ball that has backspin. The chipped ball can be played to a small space between defenders and to the attackers running into it. During a game, it is important to remember that the longer and higher the ball, the more time it takes to come down, thus giving the defense time to recover or the attacker time to reach the ball.

Long Throw-Ins

A player capable of throwing the ball over 30 yards is a valuable asset when the attackers have a throw-in in the attacking third. Since players cannot be offside on a throw-in, it can be even more effective than a corner kick because the thrower can feed the ball accurately to a teammate in a dangerous area in front of the goal.

The Goalie: Individual Offense and Defense

An attack should start immediately after the ball is won back and before the opponents can fully organize their defense. When possession is regained by the goalie, he or she usually decides what course the attack will take. The preferred course is to work the ball out by throwing it to either a defender playing wide or to a midfielder or forward who is open on a touchline. This makes it easier to retain possession, and it draws opponents in, that is, away from their own goal.

If the goalie's team is completely marked, a long punt is the best option, since over 80 percent of the defensive team will be caught far from their own goal. As the goalie punts the ball, defenders and midfielders should be moving upfield to support their forwards, who will be trying to control the punt, and possibly to force the other team's forwards and midfielders offside in the event that the punt is not controlled. The goalie should punt sparingly because it is easy to lose possession when the ball lands. (Remember that the more often possession is lost, the more energy must be used to regain it.)

As the initiator of many attacks, the goalkeeper must be a leader and should be able to make correct choices.

Defensively, the goalie must also know when to come out of the goal area and penalty area. There is no rule against this; the only limitation is that, once out of the penalty area, the goalie cannot use his or her hands. When necessary, the goalie should come out to cut off the angle of an attacker's shot, and to help and support the defenders. An immobile goalie is a bad goalie. If a goalie does use his or her hands outside the penalty area, he or she will be called for a hand ball and a direct kick on ball will be taken at the spot the infraction occurred.

Small Group Tactics

7

In building a team, the primary goal is to put together players whose individual abilities combine well, who understand each other's capabilities and tendencies, and who can play to each other's strengths and cover their weaknesses. When 2 or 3 players in adjacent positions can do this, the team will develop great efficiency in those areas, making for an outstanding season and success as long as the combination lasts.

A team is composed of 11 individuals playing in various small groups of 2 or 3, combining here and there and then passing the ball to another area where another small group takes over for a few passes. The coach must find players who complement each other to make these small groups work well with each other. Each group develops its own patterns of defense and attack, which will determine how they fit into the whole system, or what system will best accommodate them. It is the coach's responsibility to improve the performance of each particular group and to increase their effectiveness collectively.

The following sections present common patterns of play for small groups of 2 or 3 players.

Offensive Support

The receiver of a pass should have a support player to his or her side and one to the rear, providing two immediate passing options. A good exercise for this is a 3 v 3 game that allows anywhere from one to unlimited touches. The game may be played in two halves of 10–15 minutes, adjusted for age as necessary. This is a high-intensity game; players constantly change roles from backup, to support, to ball carrier. All players must constantly run for positioning or open space. (See Figure 7.1.)

Defensive Backing

Figure 7.3 a–b illustrates drills for the practice of defensive backing.

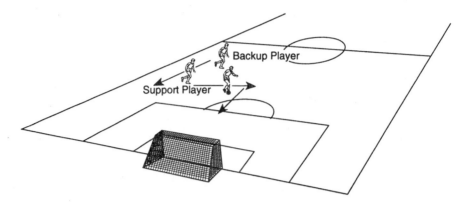

Figure 7.1
Players constantly change roles from backup to support to ball carrier in this 3 v 3 exercise. All players constantly run for positioning or open space.

Figure 7.2
A defender jockeys an opponent in possession of the ball.

Movement off the Ball

A good team never stands still. No matter who has the ball, nearby players are always moving and making runs for the teammate with the ball. This draws defenders to different positions and creates spaces for other players to receive a pass.

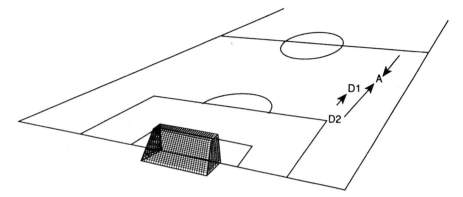

Figure 7.3a
Drills for the practice of defensive backing. A defender, D1, jockeys an attacker to stall for time. The backup, D2, moves to tackle the player with the ball while the jockeying player follows immediately, leaving the attacker no place to go. In tackling the opponent, the backup covers only half of the opponent's intended path; the other half is covered by the jockeying player.

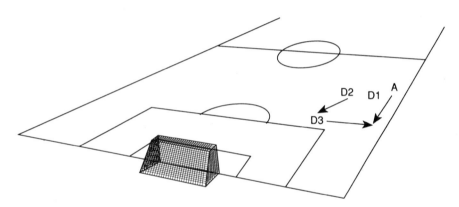

Figure 7.3b
The dribbler is forced by defensive positioning to go to the outside, where D3 can intercept, while D2 takes the place of D3. (Defensive rotation)

Forcing the Play

While a defender is practicing the delaying tactic (see Figure 7.2), another defender moves to support and cover the defense's most vulnerable area, *forcing* the attacker toward a less dangerous area. This gives the defense more time and forces more predictable reactions by the attackers. (See Figure 7.4.)

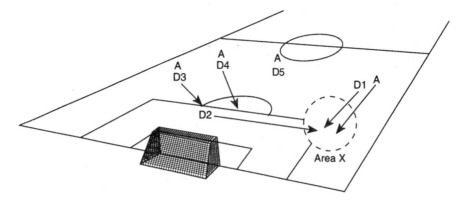

Figure 7.4
D1 jockeys the ball carrier, who is forced wide, while D2 moves up to support. When D2 is close to D1 in area X, D1 will attempt to take the ball or wait for D2 to attack. D3 and D4 drop further back.

The Offside Trap

A quick thrust by the attackers can catch the defense unprepared and at a numerical disadvantage. In this case, the last defender (usually the sweeper) pushes his or her teammates up by moving forward quickly, putting one or more attackers in an offside position.

This is a dangerous maneuver, since the last defender must anticipate both the moment and direction of the opponents' pass and coordinate the defense at the same time. It all takes place in a split second, demanding a fine sense of timing. Even then, the referee or linesman may not be in the right position to call the offside thus giving a breakaway to the attackers and an almost sure goal.

The Indirect Attack

An indirect attack includes a series of plays that advance slowly in one area of the field with the real intent of scoring from another area.

If the attackers are working the ball on the right side, they will draw the defense to that side and the probability of breaking through to the goal on that side becomes very low. Once the defense is drawn, the ball should be played across the field, forcing the defense to shift. Once this is accomplished, the ball should again be switched to the original side.

This double shift confuses and tires the defense, causing physical and mental errors that may lead to a goal. If the defense expects the switch and covers both areas, they will be spread out enough to allow penetration through the middle of the field.

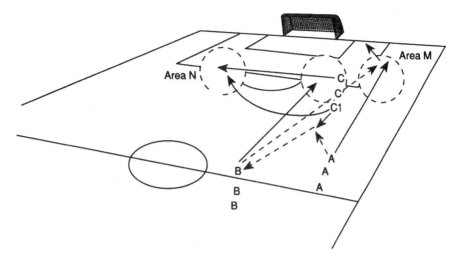

Figure 7.5

Near-post runs. C1 *moves to receive* the pass from A and then passes to B, who *comes to meet* the ball. B passes (chip pass) to area M where A has moved to receive a pass. C1 moves for support in line with the far post. B moves to assist A at the near post.

Near-Post Runs

On attack, players are encouraged to dribble the ball to the near post and play the ball to the far post. This is termed *near-post/far-post play variation.* The general idea is to work the attack toward the goal line and come as close as possible to the near post before passing or shooting. This forces the defense to shift, leaving the far-post area with fewer defenders. A pass to this area can then give the attacking forward a one-on-one situation with the possibility of an open goal. This move is best learned with the basic drill seen in Figure 7.5, eventually adding one or two defenders and ending with a shot on goal.

In conducting this drill with defenders, the attackers approaching the goal line to the right or left of the goal should move as close to an upright as possible. When the defender is drawn out, the pass should be made diagonally back to the area in front of the near or far post. The closer the post, the more sharply the pass should be angled. Support players can place themselves approximately in line with each upright and 5–15 yards behind the passer.

Many players look to beat a defender and then pass, rather than passing after drawing the defender out. A player should only pass the ball after dribbling to the near post if he or she is unable to score. After passing, the original dribbler should not remain in an offside position, which will happen if the receiver does not shoot but makes another pass instead. The original dribbler should move to a support position that is not offside.

A general drill to accustom players to near-post runs is provided by adding a goalie to the exercise in Figure 7.5. Once the basic concept is understood and the players have learned how to vary their passes and positions according to the goalie's reactions, a defender is introduced to assist the goalie. After the attackers begin to compensate for the many variables introduced by this addition, a second defender is added. This exercise challenges players to find new options and provides the game-like experience of penetrating in front of the goal.

Change of Pace

Change of pace means slowing down the game then speeding it up; it can be done by an individual or by a group of players. It is effective because the defensive team cannot keep its own rhythm. When the defense relaxes because the game has slowed down, the attackers should increase the pace, catching them unprepared for a quick passing combination downfield that will penetrate their defensive third.

Team Communication

Assume that teammates can only communicate among themselves with the spoken word. What if there is a lot of noise from spectators, thunder, or loudspeakers? How does a player distinguish between a teammate and an opponent whose voice sounds similar—assuming that the voices can even be heard? While concentrating on the game, some players have trouble hearing and distinguishing voices right next to them.

Positional sense, vision, timing, moving into space, and other skills are important in soccer. How can players develop these skills if someone is always telling them what to do? When will they stop depending on their teammates? How will they manage with new teammates, possibly from different soccer backgrounds or different countries?

In unusual situations, talking may help, but young people must be taught not to depend on others to keep them aware of the flow of play. Calling for a ball can be a good decoy, but an earnest call is often counterproductive: an alert opponent can certainly assess the situation and intervene. Calling for the ball alerts the defense and often renders the pass useless.

But suppose that a player develops expressions that only his or her teammates can understand—a sort of team code. Teams can have prearranged and well-rehearsed set plays for dead-ball situations as well as moving plays for various areas of the field. Certain signals can be used to communicate intention.

The direction of a pass can tell a teammate where to turn, where a defender is, etc. Likewise, a teammate's run can communicate where he or she wants a pass, or it can be a dummy run to make space for another teammate. The specific forms of communication are not important, but it is essential that team members understand each others' intentions.

When players have worked together for a long time, they can often read each other's intentions and anticipate moves. This is the most important aspect of teamwork. No matter how hard players work to develop cohesion among teammates, time and individual understanding seem to be the most important factors in creating it.

The Meaning of a Pass

The ball is passed to a teammate when and where it can best be utilized, depending on the position of the defending players. A good rule to remember is to make the first sure pass that presents itself. This may slow down an attack, but the team will not lose possession.

Accurate passing is important for many reasons. First, continually chasing down bad passes can wear a teammate out unnecessarily. Second, a player risks injury when pushing to win a 50–50 ball against a defender who will tackle hard to win it. Finally, and most obviously, a bad pass often results in losing possession, and the team will have to work twice as hard to win the ball back.

Playing the Blind Side and the Blind-Side Pass

The blind-side pass is played to the space beyond the defender, where he or she must turn and then run for the ball. The attacker, who is already facing that direction, has the advantage. The defender must depend on teammates for backup. If there is a mix-up in communication and no defender is there to cover, the pass becomes very risky.

In Figure 7.6, M passes to area X; D1 must turn 180 degrees to run for the ball. F1 runs forward without turning. F2 can also run to space X if F1 does not. If any defender hesitates, F1 or F2 will have possession in their attacking third of the field. In anticipating the pass F1 should be in line with D1.

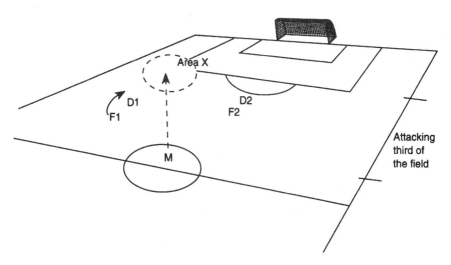

Figure 7.6
Playing the blind side.

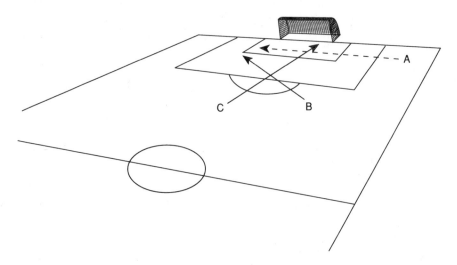

Figure 7.7
Cross pass with positional exchange. A crosses the ball, C makes a near-post run, and B runs wide for support. If C does not receive the ball well, he or she will let it go for B.

Exchanging Positions

Exchanging positions with a teammate is an effective way to confuse defenders who are accustomed to covering particular players. The defender who follows his or her player after the exchange will be playing out of position; by staying, however, the defender will be covering an unfamiliar player. In either case, the defender's chance of making errors increases. (See Figure 7.7.)

Stretching the Defense

A good way to stretch the defense is to have the wings play wide on the touchlines in the middle third. This draws the opposing defenders into those areas and gives the wings more space in back of the defenders to run after a lead pass, after possession is won. The stopper will have to stay in the middle before the pass is made; otherwise, if the stopper goes to one side in anticipation, the pass will go to the other side and well beyond the defense. This tactic is particularly effective if a team has very fast wings. Figure 7.8 presents a drill for stretching the defense in the attacking end.

Wall Passes

The most common example of small group tactics is the wall pass, which involves two players trying to beat one defender. The defender's position determines whether a diagonal pass or a through pass will be used. (See Figures 7.9 and 7.10.)

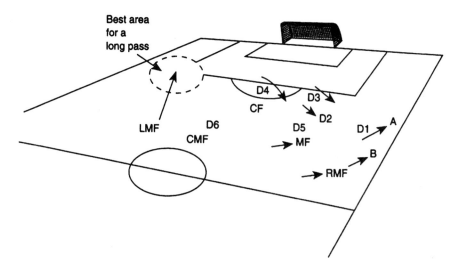

Figure 7.8
Stretching the defense wide. The right and left wings, A and B, go wide on the same side. The right midfielder (RMF) follows B for support. Defenders 1 and 2 move accordingly. The danger area is thinly covered. The LMF and MF move to meet a probable pass. A pass is made to the space while receivers approach the periphery of the area where the pass will be made. Both passes and runs must be *timed.* If the defense does not follow, go to the line and the near post. This should open up the far-post area.

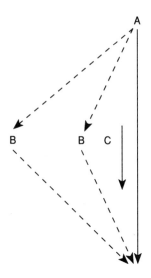

Figure 7.9
The basic wall pass. A passes to B and runs to receive a return pass. This is known as the wall pass (or a touch-and-go pass) because B acts as a wall, returning the ball to A in the direction in which it would have bounced had it bounced off a wall.

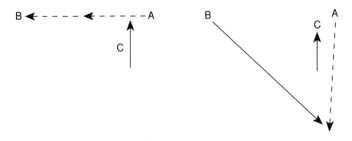

Figure 7.10
Left: A pass from A to B would be dangerous, because a running C could intercept. Right: To prevent C from intercepting, A makes a pass to the outside of C and B runs diagonally to receive the pass.

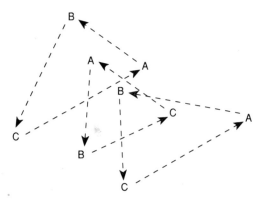

Figure 7.11
Moving, free form, passes of three. Each group of three players passes the ball in sequence (A to B to C to A, etc.) while not running into either of the other groups. Each player must find the intended receiver in a crowd. The number of groups and the area assigned vary according to skill level. Players are forced to look ahead of the ball and to run for open spaces.

The Triangle Formation

Another basic tactic is the triangle formation (Figure 7.11). This is especially effective when players interchange positions and observe predetermined passing sequences. For instance, player A passes to B, who passes to C, who passes back to A again—all the while changing positions and moving forward.

A similar pattern involves passes among four players: A to B to C to D and D back to A. The interchanging of positions confuses the defense, while attackers know who the receivers will be and who will run where. Different passing combinations should be used to increase unpredictability and stimulate player creativity. Whatever combination is used, it should be geared to an attack on the goal. Every pass that is not geared to attacking the goal decreases the chance of scoring.

Takeovers

In a *takeover,* a shielding player, while moving laterally across the field, leaves the ball so an approaching teammate can take it over and turn it toward the goal. This maneuver brings two marking defenders together, obstructing (and thus neutralizing) one and allowing for penetration by both attackers. In addition, the player who took the ball over can backpass to a support player, who can then chip it forward to one of the two original players who are making diagonal runs toward the goal.

Shielding the ball and takeovers confuse the defenders. If they hesitate to sort out the confusion, the attackers can exploit the moment and penetrate the defense. Shielding and takeovers in an opponent's penalty box create a dangerous situation for the other team to deal with. Since soccer is a percentage game, the chances are good that the offensive team will score in those situations.

Figures 7.12 and 7.13 demonstrate takeover situations. In Figure 7.12, Player A, in possession, shields the ball from the defender as B approaches. In Figure 7.13, B takes the ball from A and cuts diagonally toward the goal line, drawing the sweeper. Player A cuts toward the goal line on the complementary diagonal. A diagonal pass from B to A will also eliminate the sweeper from the play.

This exchange is especially effective when both A and B are being tightly marked. What happens in this case is that B's defender is neutralized when B takes the ball from A, being obstructed by A or A's defender. When the play is properly executed, B gains a few seconds freedom from tight coverage.

The takeover is even more effective when two forwards play against three defenders. It can take place on any part of the field and work either laterally or up and down the field.

Covering for the Goalie

Sometimes the goalie must leave part of the goal unprotected, necessitating the assistance of teammates. For example, if an opponent breaks through the defense and is attacking the near post, the goalie must come out to intercept and cut off the shooting angle, leaving the goal open. A defender should drop back and cover the goal as well as possible. Any nearby player, usually a fullback, takes the goalie's position while other players mark open attackers.

On a corner kick or a cross pass where the goalie goes out to catch the ball, defenders should again move back to protect the goal area.

The Overlap

When a player moves upfield beyond the teammates who would normally be positioned in front of him or her, it is called an *overlap.* Most overlaps are executed by the defenders, who are highlighted in the following paragraphs. It helps to

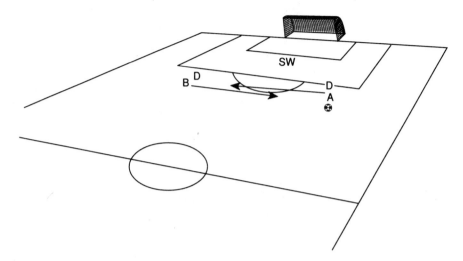

Figure 7.12
A takeover situation (followed by Figure 7.13).

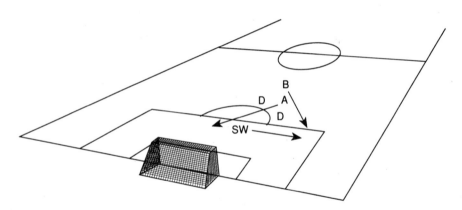

Figure 7.13
A takeover situation.

have a very fast fullback who is versatile enough to play like a midfielder or a wing but who can retreat quickly if possession is lost.

The play commonly begins when the opposition's defense is drawn to one side of the field in the middle third or their defensive third. If the defense covers the right wing moving toward the center, the space on the right touchline is the overlap area and the play is termed an *outside overlap* (Figure 7.14). If the forward stays wide, then the back goes for the area leading to the near post. This is called an *inside overlap*.

Normally two or three passes are made by the midfielders to allow the overlapping back time to advance. When the back overlaps, it is often tactically *necessary* that he or she receive a pass. For example, in Figure 7.14, if midfielder 1

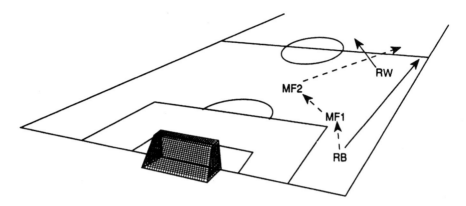

Figure 7.14
The outside overlap: The right defensive back (RB) passes to a midfielder before running up the right touchline. The receiving midfielder passes to another midfielder, allowing the back time to advance. The second midfielder makes a high or low pass, as necessary, to the back in the overlap area (note the right wing (RW) run). If more time is required for the back to advance to the overlap area, a third pass among the midfielders may be added.

attempts a short lateral pass to the left, the back will not be utilized and, if the pass is inaccurate, the back will be caught too far upfield to recover. A long forward diagonal cross-field pass would not be too dangerous; if possession is lost, there is still some time to recover the ball.

If, by this overlap, the back can draw out the sweeper or another defender needed in the middle of the field, and can draw him or her before the pass is made, then the team can use the overlapping back as a decoy and make another play toward the far post.

It should be noted that spontaneity is essential; the less expected the overlapping move, the greater its chance for success. When using a 4–4–2 or a 3–5–2 system, overlaps by the fullbacks and outside midfielders are almost mandatory if a team is going to play attacking soccer. Without it, the attack is much more predictable and conservative and thus less likely to result in a goal.

The following drills are designed to facilitate teamwork among small groups of players.

Drills of Two

In Figure 7.15, A feeds passes to B in such a way as to make B move from side to side like a pendulum. To make this drill or any of its variations more demanding, increase the distance between the two players and/or the speed of execution.

Variations:

1. A moves forward as B backs up.
2. B faces away from A and must turn to pass back to A while A advances.

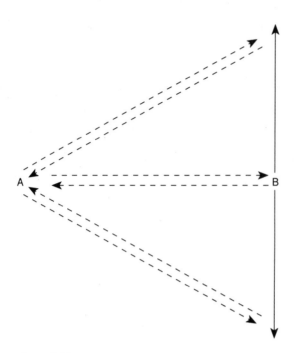

Figure 7.15
Drills of two.

3. B is stationary, and A feeds underhand, gentle, waist-high passes to B.
4. B returns high head balls thrown by A.
5. A volleys to B, keeping the ball off the ground.
6. A moves backward as B advances.
7. A passes to B from 10 yards away, using the side of the foot with one touch only.
8. A passes to B; B changes the ball to the other foot and passes back.
9. Same as 8, but using the instep.
10. Same as 8, but increasing the distance to 30 yards and sending high balls.

Drills of Three

A passes to C, C returns the pass to A; A then chips the ball to B. B passes to C, C returns the pass to B; B then chips the ball to A; and so on (see Figure 7.16).
Variations:

1. Instead of a chip, A passes wide to C, who meets and passes the ball to B using one or two touches.
2. A chips a ball wide over C's head; C controls and passes back to B. B passes to C on the ground; C passes back to B, and B chips again over C's head.

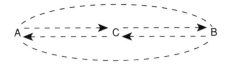

Figure 7.16
Drills of three.

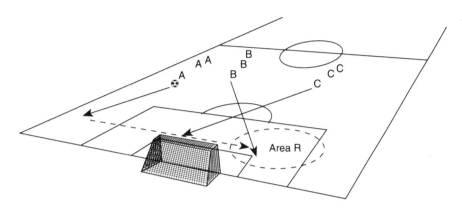

Figure 7.17
Positional exchange with shots on goal.

3. C receives and turns with the ball to pass to B, using one touch to turn the ball and one touch to pass it.
4. The pass to C should be fast and hard to control. This makes C learn to turn and pass difficult balls as might occur in a game.
5. The players are close to each other, using up to three touches. The ball should not touch the ground.

Figure 7.17 demonstrates a positional exchange with shots on goal. The first player from group A dribbles the ball to the goal line and makes a fast cross pass, on the ground or in the air, to area R. The first B and the first C run to the respectively opposite post. If A's pass cannot be handled well by C at the near-post area, C lets it go for B in the far-post area. Either B or C takes a shot on goal.

Figure 7.18 illustrates another drill of three. In this drill, the first player in group A dribbles to the goal line before making a long cross to area R. The first B runs to receive the pass and, with a one-touch pass, sets up C, who is moving in for a shot. Distances may be varied and passes made slower or faster, as necessary.

In Figure 7.19, players exchange positions while weaving and passing (this drill may or may not end with a shot on goal).

Figures 7.20, 7.21, and 7.22 illustrate other drills of three.

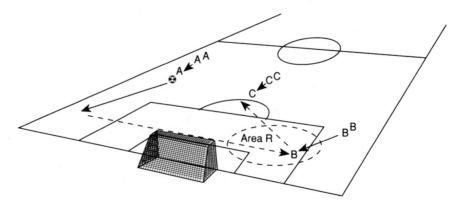

Figure 7.18
Another drill of three.

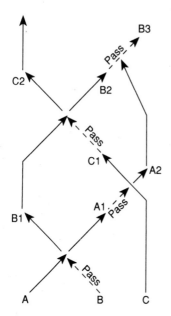

Figure 7.19
Exchanging positions.

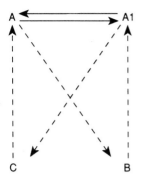

Figure 7.20
Player A passes to B and runs to position A1 for a return pass; A then passes to C and runs back to the original position for a return pass. In a variation, A passes to B, who is under pressure from C. Player B shields the ball and attempts to turn on C before passing back to A.

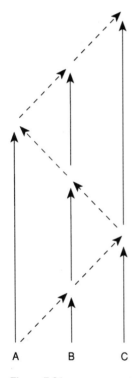

Figure 7.21
Three players run back and forth along imaginary straight lines and at an even pace. Passers must time their teammates' runs in order to make passes that can be taken in stride. Only one touch is allowed. Even speeds and parallel lines must be maintained to force accurately timed leading passes.

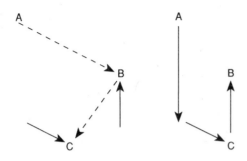

Figure 7.22
Left: A passes to B, who comes to meet the ball, while C moves to receive a pass from B. After passing, A moves to the open space vacated by C. Moving for the ball forces positional exchange. Right: Note the new positioning of the three players, with C and A in front and B to the back. Continue passing and switching positions.

Drills of Four

1. In a grid or a free space, 3 v 1 keep-away.
2. A game of 2 v 2 with shots of goal, lasting five minutes.
3. A game of 1 v 1 for one minute before giving the ball to the remaining two players for one minute's play.
4. Four players with two balls, passing to the free players.
5. Four players with three balls, passing to the free player.
6. A game of 3 v 1 to goal and ending with an outside shot. The shot must be taken from outside the penalty area.
7. Inside and outside overlapping drills.

Team Tactics

Complementary Play

No matter how skilled and versatile a particular player is, a team performs best when the defense, midfield, and offense are comprised of individuals with a *variety* of exceptional qualities. Every player has something outstanding to offer. During a long season, these individual qualities, properly blended into the team, will surface when needed and help win games.

Players need to know each other's strengths and attempt to put them to use during games. Conversely, it is also important to compensate for individual weaknesses. A very good dribbler may be assisted by a backup player who briefly influences the defender to move in a position more advantageous to the dribbler. This might prevent the defender from committing a foul and stopping the attack. Or the same dribbler, with a backup, can pull out the defender and the sweeper, thus creating at least a one-on-one situation in front of the goal, where the ball will be crossed by the dribbler or the backup. Several one-on-one situations between a defender and an outstanding receiver can force an error and thus produce a score. Remember, play the percentage game!

Possession

If your team controls the ball, obviously the other team does not. In a 90-minute game, the ball is in play an average of 60 minutes. A team that controls the ball for as long as possible handicaps the opposition, because goals are rarely scored without extensive time of possession.

Controlling the ball requires practice. When scoring chances are remote, keep possession and try again when a good opportunity presents itself. This can be successfully practiced in keep-away drills utilizing a "conversion" player, who plays on whichever team happens to have the ball. The object is to make as many passes as possible without losing control. This teaches patience.

A drill useful for similar purposes is presented in Figure 8.1. This drill teaches several basic concepts: possession, patience, and regrouping (playing the ball back to the defense before starting a new attack if the first one does not look promising). It teaches players to defend and counterattack, and to switch the game

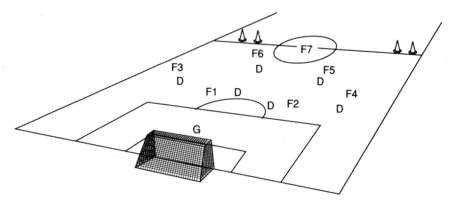

Figure 8.1
A game of 7 v 7 with three goals.

from side to side on the field, supporting and backing up the teammate with the ball.

This drill should be used extensively since it simulates a game situation and teaches the overlapping technique for the defense, as well as changing the game from one side to the other in the middle third of the field. The forwards learn to defend immediately as soon as possession is lost.

Game Rhythm

When mentally mature enough (ages 14–15), players should be taught different ways to play the game. Variations in pace make the players think about their approach and stimulate their creative processes. During a game, a team must establish a certain tempo of play, or rhythm, speeding up or slowing down according to the situation. Most teams have high and low moments during games. If they score during the highs, of course, their chances of winning are very good. In that case, the defense's task is to slow them down or break their momentum. This can be done by crowding, using delaying tactics, and especially by playing keep-away to maintain possession. Opponents become unnerved and discouraged when they cannot get a foot on the ball. They will become impatient and make mistakes that can be exploited.

The following are a few examples that can be used to accustom players to the concept of change of rhythm and help them adjust as necessary.

1. After your side scores a goal, the opposition will try even harder to score. This is the time to win the ball and play a few minutes of keep-away. This is very discouraging to the opponents, who will likely dissipate their intensity by chasing the ball around the field.
2. When time is of the utmost importance, pressure the opponent all over the field, playing without a sweeper to regain possession. This must happen when your team is one goal or more down.

3. When ahead, or even if the game is tied, defend only on your half of the field; in other words, play low-pressure defense. This forces the opponent to attack and push players up, leaving more space in the defensive end for your eventual counter attack.
4. Play a zone defense and switch to a tight, partial "man-to-man" defense as the opposition comes closer to your goal line. Bring midfielders back to cover any players who aren't covered when moving out of their zone.
5. Slow down the pace when playing back-to-back games, as happens in a tournament. Make medium-length passes that require less running. This gives teammates time to recover and conserve strength.

Drawing out the Defense

To draw out the opposing defense, the attackers should play back in their own half. This entices the opposing defenders to gradually move forward, with the intention of gaining possession. As they move forward, one of the attacking midfielders or forwards drops back to receive the ball. If he or she is followed by an opponent, the plan is working.

As the opponent moves forward, he or she vacates space that can be exploited. A pass is made to the vacated space for another attacker, who in turn goes for goal in order to draw another defender.

Basically, this move is designed to tease the opposition into thinking they can win the ball by advancing out from their goal. An advancing defense leaves more space behind it, and this space should be looked for and exploited.

Overcrowding

Let's now look at the same situation from the defender's point of view. Against highly skilled attacking teams, the defending *forwards and midfielders* are brought back in a small area around the opposing team's attack. This causes overcrowding, which leads to loss of possession or a change of pattern. The attackers will be forced to make a 40- to 50-yard pass to a different area of the field, buying time (3–4 seconds) for the defense. The defensive team should anticipate this and be prepared to intercept.

If the offensive team insists on going through this cluster of defenders, who usually form a triangle or diamond pattern, they will lose the ball. What makes this effective is the offensive team's lack of tactical knowledge. At the least, this triangle or diamond defensive midfield formation slows down the attack, so the immediate defense is ready and "negative players" can come back to help. (A *negative player* is one who is behind the ball on offense or in front of the ball on defense.)

A good example of this principle is the 3–5–2 system now widely used in the U.S. The 4–4–2 and 3–5–2 systems of play lend themselves to this style of defense (see Figure 8.2).

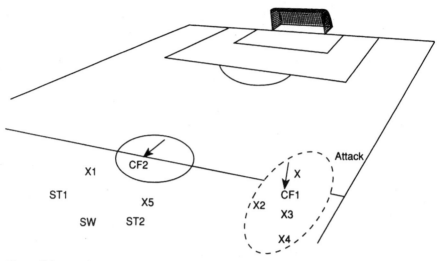

Figure 8.2
Crowding the zone. All players: ST1, ST2, SW, X1, CF1 and CF2 are from the same defensive team.

Avoiding the Accordion Game

An attacking team should be compact, not stretched out like an accordion as in Figure 8.3. If a forward moves rapidly with the ball toward the goal while his or her defense is walking, the field is covered too thinly, making it harder to recover if possession is lost. Team leaders must close this gap by pushing up the defense and midfielders, while providing the attacking forwards with backup. Teams should move in *blocks* defensively and offensively. The distance from the farthest attacking forward to the deepest defender, excluding the goalie, should never be more than 50–60 yards. This makes it easier to recover, back up a play, or find a teammate. It also makes runs for the ball shorter, which means less overall running.

Pulling the Sweeper

Because the sweeper is the only defender without individual coverage responsibility, he or she must be forced out of the middle (see Figure 8.4). If a team attacks, for instance, on the right side, the sweeper will come out to back up the corresponding outside back, *especially if the attacker has a backup.* This creates a brief two-on-one situation against the outside back, making penetration very probable. Once the sweeper is drawn out, the other defenders are left, at best, with one-on-one situations. Any of the attacking players will then have a better chance to beat a defender or at least gain one or two steps, enabling a pass or shot. (The attackers must remember to pass the ball outside the goalie's reach. The goalie, seeing the sweeper going out, should anticipate a cross.)

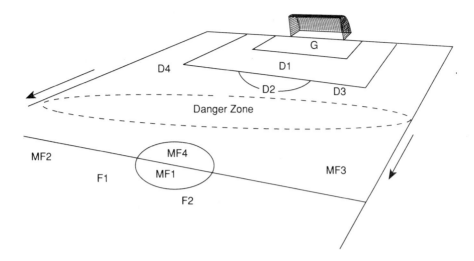

Figure 8.3
The accordion effect—caused by defense lagging behind fast moving forwards. The accordion concept: In this diagram, the defenders are slow to move forward while the forwards have rapidly moved downfield, leaving dangerous open space between. The defenders should move forward quickly to cover the open space.

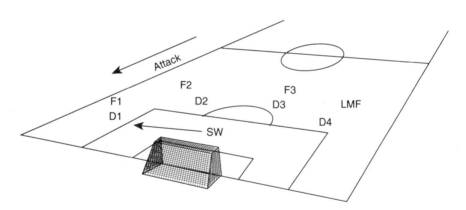

Figure 8.4
Pulling the sweeper. The sweeper or libero must back up D1, in case F1 is able to beat D1. This leaves F2, F3, and LMF (left midfielder) in one-on-one situations.

If the sweeper chooses to remain in the center, then a midfielder or even a forward should drop back to support the outside fullback.

Pressuring the attackers demands increased skill, vision, and anticipation; that is why clearing the ball from the area is recommended for less skilled players. The clear resolves a difficult situation and reduces the chance for error and being scored on.

Counterattack

As soon as possession is won, a plan for counterattack should be utilized. The coach should designate certain key players, capable of deciding the best direction of an attack and initiating it, to receive the ball. These players are usually quite skilled, with good vision and some creativity. This advance planning is necessary because there is very little time—usually less than four seconds—to initiate a successful counterattack. After four seconds, the opponent's defense will be set up and surprise will be lost. Counterattacks should be rehearsed so that all players understand who should be where.

In the defensive third. After gaining possession in the defensive third, the player preparing a counterattack should try to dribble the ball to an open space, then look to play the ball diagonally forward. (See Figure 8.5.) The more opponents (negative players) are left behind the ball in a quick counterattack, the greater probability of success. The predetermined receiver will, in turn, give a long pass directly forward, over the defense, or make a short pass to retain possession if the attack is not organized. The short pass allows the attackers to draw the defense, which will open up space for another diagonal forward pass across the field, forcing them to shift again. As they are shifting, a pass is made to the space on the opposite side. This constant shifting increases the chances for defensive errors and establishes a 2 v 2 or a 2 v 1 for the offensive team, making a score more likely.

In the middle third. The same basic principle applies when a counterattack begins from the middle third of the field: go for space, draw opponents, then play the ball into the space behind the defense. This space may be laterally across the field, diagonally across, or straight through (for which a *through ball* is named). The pass should go where the defense is most vulnerable. If moving the ball to the right, a player and his or her teammates should be expecting the ball to be played to the left side of the field. In short, "Play right, think left" (see Figure 8.6).

Moving for the pass, the receiver will draw two defenders, one of which will be the sweeper. With the help of a backup, the receiving forward could go to the goal line and attempt to penetrate to the post. If this is not possible, a pass can be made to the backup, who then makes a cross to the far-post area or to teammates who should be making runs to the near-post and far-post areas.

In the attacking third. In this case, whoever wins the ball goes for goal or shoots if possible. One option is to dribble to the post, or to the goal line and then to the post. This draws the defense and the goalie to that side and alerts the attacker's teammates to a possible pass to the near post or a chip to the far post.

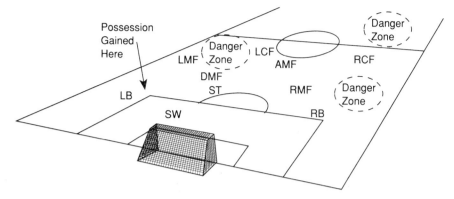

Figure 8.5
Counterattack from the defensive third. The ball is won over in the defensive third. The three areas dangerous to the opposition are clearly visible. The chip or high passes are most effective.

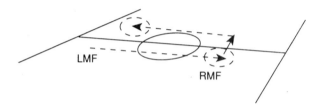

Figure 8.6
Counterattack from the middle third. Possession is gained in the middle third. The ball is crossed to the opposite side of the field, where an attacker dribbles for penetration before crossing it again.

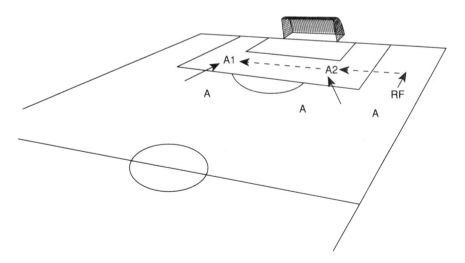

Figure 8.7
Counterattack in the attacking third. The receivers, A1 and A2, have backups and are ready to receive a pass to near- or far-post areas.

The attacker's teammates should position themselves in the fringe areas (see Figure 8.7), to either meet the pass and end with a shot on goal or make another pass to an open player if there is no clear shot. Defenses naturally tend to be in line with the attack and drift to that side, allowing some space where attacking forwards can take a successful shot.

Total and Partial Pressure

Also known as *pressure defense,* total and partial pressure are used to regain possession of the ball and to prevent an opposing team's attempt to gain time for positioning. When the opposing goalie has the ball, all other opposing players should be covered. This gives the goalie no choice but to punt the ball, which should be easily won by the defenders.

The same pressure can be applied if the opposing goalie throws an outlet pass to one of the outside fullbacks. When the fullback receives the ball, everyone covers a player (the goalie is covered as well), denying the fullback a passing target. The fullback now either must make a long pass to remove the ball from pressure, make a short pass under pressure, or dribble while under pressure. In either case, the chances are good that the opposing team will lose the ball.

Three methods can be used to create *total pressure* against another team:

1. Two opponents who are in close proximity and far removed from the goalie (50–60 yards away) can be covered by a single defender, who can intercept a pass intended for either one.
2. Players move up one position such that the sweeper also covers a player. The defense then arrays itself as in the WM system (see chapter 11), with the backs covering one-on-one and anticipating help only from each other, not from the sweeper.
3. As soon as a ball is lost, all players run fast to defend their own half or last third of the field. This utilizes the overcrowding principle and is extremely effective against superior teams. This principle can also be applied in certain zones of the field to stop an attack and regain possession. This style is actually a low-pressure defense because it allows the opposing team to build up their attack. But when the attackers reach the other team's defensive half, the pressure picks up into a high-intensity defense that can deliver a quick counterattack since most of the opponents have been tricked into pulling up.

Principles of Attack

9

The field is divided into three equal sections. The *defensive third* is the section in front of a team's goal. The *middle third* is the middle of the field or the section in front of a team's defensive third. The *attacking third*—sometimes called the *offensive third*—is the section in front of a team's middle third, which is also the opposing team's defensive third.

To be sucessful in attacking, a team must be able to control the ball in the opposition's half of the field and create useful space in the attacking third. The transition from defense to a quick attack should take less than four seconds. If a team cannot initiate, direct, and start executing the last phase of an attack within this time, the opportunity will pass. Even if possession is retained, the attack will be slow, giving the defense time to get set, and scoring will be more difficult and will require greater skill.

In the defensive third, the attack should start from the backs. The goalie passes to defenders who are placed wide, outside of the penalty area and in front of the goal line. Once received, the ball is passed laterally by the backs, with the intent of drawing the opposing forwards (F) and spreading them apart. If this succeeds, defender D1, with the ball, splits the forwards by either advancing with the ball between two forwards (as in Figure 9.1), or passing it to any teammate B, who comes back and *shows*—that is, makes himself or herself available for a pass—in a free space in the middle third of the field. Player B will not be free for long, perhaps a couple of seconds, so another teammate, C—in this case, probably a midfielder—should move up to support. This gives B someone to pass to if a defensive player makes it impossible to turn upfield with the ball.

Ideally, receiver B should pass the ball back if a support player is available because the support player is facing in the direction of the attack and can see the whole field, while B, whose back is turned, cannot. Now B can turn without the ball and support player C, who just received the pass. While these quick passes, called *one-two combinations,* are going on, another player, D, probably from the attacking third of the field, should show for player C. A teammate on the opposite side of the field, from any one of the thirds, should move into the place last occupied by C.

The above is not a set play to be repeated every time an attack starts from the defensive third. What is important here are the principles: support, pass, move, show. It is easy to defend against a stagnant team because communication is easy to maintain among the defenders who are marking opposing players. However,

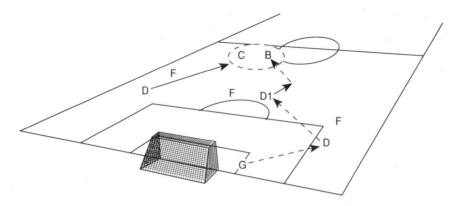

Figure 9.1
Attacking from the defensive third.

when a team is in constant motion it becomes difficult to know who is marking whom. The pace of the game becomes much quicker, and there is less time to think and communicate changes.

If the receiver of a pass does not get support, the message is clear: turn and either dribble and beat the opponent or pass to another area if possible. If neither of these options is open, the ball should be passed back safely to a defender or back to the goalie, either of whom can restart the attack from a different area. This is a much better option for a receiver who does not know what to do with the ball before receiving it, instead of trying to turn blindly upfield and risk losing possession. Once possession is lost, more time and energy must be spent on regaining it and then starting an attack all over again.

Here are some guidelines for building an attack:

1. Generally, a forward or midfielder should not turn with the ball when covered unless there is time to do so. By glancing backward while showing for the ball, the player will have an idea of where teammates and opponents are. The teammate who passes the ball can also give a verbal instruction by yelling something like "man on!" (there's a player on your back) or "turn outside!" (turn to the outside).

   The teammate's pass can also convey *nonverbal* instructions. A pass to the outside of the receiver means there is a defender on the inside, and vice versa. A fast pass to the feet means "turn." A slower short pass that the receiver must run back for indicates that there is a player on his or her back.
2. Depending on the defender's position, the ball should be passed into a space for the showing player to run to. Players should never receive a ball while stationary, but should always run to meet the ball. The receiver who waits for the ball gives the defender more time to intercept.
3. After collecting the ball, the receiver should always pass to someone facing the play.

4. Any player receiving a pass must also have support players for backup, in case a defender blindsides and tackles him or her, and to increase the attack's probability of success.
5. Most players tend to drift to the side of the field where the ball is in play (the "strong side"). The other team's defense will shift to that side to even up the ratio of defensive to offensive players. This means that the opposite side, or *weak side*, of the field is open. Once the defensive team is drawn to the strong side, the play should be switched to the weak side.

Attacking the Weak Side—Stretching the Defense

Since the offensive team knows when its members are going to switch the ball to the weak side, they should have a player holding wide, staying almost literally on the touchline on the opposite side and making a run up the field for a lead pass. This causes the defense to break down, and it gives the offensive team both a numerical advantage and space to develop a shot on goal.

It is important that the ball be switched when a teammate on the weak side makes a run upfield; otherwise the defending team will win the ball back and be in position to feed their own weak-side player (who has been left open by the attacker's run upfield).

Most modern defenses have a stopper and a sweeper in the middle of their defensive third. In the attacking third, the offensive team should try to draw the defending sweeper to the strong side before switching the ball. Once this is accomplished, a long pass should be directed to the weak side, forcing the sweeper or goalie to shift, then another pass should be made back to the original area, where the shifting of the defense has created a numerical superiority for the offense. Penetration through a numerically superior defense is impractical—and nearly impossible against any decently organized defense. The more times the ball is switched, the greater the possibility of defensive error.

The main ingredient in creating scoring bids is patience. Control of the ball must be maintained, and potential receivers must patiently wait in, or run to, appropriate spaces to receive passes. When the numerically superior defense is drawn to the strong side, a weak-side teammate can score from the weak side.

Remember: patience and control. Do not give the ball away. A goal cannot be scored against a team that has possession of the ball.

Playing under Pressure and without Pressure

The following section presents recommended tactics for playing in the three sections of the field. They are *principles* from which plays can be developed, not set patterns to be played every time. Playing "under pressure" means playing in traffic.

Playing under Pressure

Fullbacks, on offense in the defensive third

- Do not make short passes (5–10 yards) while moving up the field to attack. If possession is lost, your defense will not be set up and will thus be very vulnerable.
- Do not try to dribble out of this area if it is congested. It is easy to get stripped of the ball here.
- Do not try to make a pass across the goal mouth (directly in front of the goal). It is too easy for an opposing player to step out and intercept the pass, especially a bad pass. The result is an almost certain goal.

Fullbacks, on defense in the defensive third

- If you do not have possession, then at least do not let the other team get organized in your defensive third. Try to intercept and get rid of the ball by clearing it out of the area, high, wide, or out of bounds.
- Delay and/or contain an oncoming attacker so teammates have time to return to defend their defensive third. Do not let the attacker dictate what happens with the ball. *Force the play;* that is, make the attacker do what you want. It is not always necessary to tackle and win the ball from the attacker. Do not try to force a tackle to win the ball and give up a foul; a good team will be very dangerous taking free kicks in the defensive third.
- Force the attacker to either pass or dribble the ball to the outside of the field and down the touchlines. Position yourself at an angle between the attacker and the goal, so that to beat you the attacker must either go the way you allow or cut across your path, in which case you should be able to tackle and win the ball. This is called *channeling* (or *jockeying*). It limits the attacker's space and helps the backup defender anticipate where the attacker will move or pass.
- If the defenders are outnumbered and cannot delay, contain, or jockey oncoming attackers, force the attackers into an offside position by having the entire defense run forward, at the same time and as quickly as possible, so that the offsides line is suddenly behind an attacker. If this tactic is timed properly, the attacker should be called offside. This is the *offside trap* discussed in chapter 7.

The offside trap should be used sparingly because good teams can easily break it by having midfielders or fullbacks, who are onside, run through the trap. They will not be called offside if they were onside when their teammate played the ball. Further, with your defense pulled forward and therefore not backing each other up, the attacking player will have a clear path to the goal if not called offside. Sometimes officials are not positioned properly and will not be able to see the offside.

Midfielders, on offense in the middle third

- Always check back to give the ball carrier another passing option. After receiving a pass from the *defensive* third, play the ball back to a support player and then move to give that player another option for an *outlet pass.* Do not try to turn with the ball; if you lose possession your defense will be outnumbered and not set up to defend against a sudden counterattack.
- Always look for support players while running into open space (or at least an area with fewer players). By moving constantly, you force the opposing team's defense to readjust continually to your position. This can create space for a teammate without the ball or for a teammate running to receive a pass. Gain as much ground as possible.
- Always run to meet a pass; never wait for it to reach you.

Midfielders, on defense in the middle third

- When possible, find a player to mark and stay no more than three feet away.
- If there are not enough players in the area to mark the attackers one on one, run to cover a dangerous space (also called *covering a zone*) in order to slow down an attack or delay an outlet pass by the other team.

Forwards, on offense in the attacking third

- Try to beat a defender so that a second defender must pick you up as you dribble toward the goal. When this happens, a teammate should be free for a pass. Taking the defender on also increases the probability that the defender will foul you while trying to steal the ball and thus give your team a free kick. This is called *forcing a foul.*
- In a breakaway situation, the ball dribbler should run for the near post and a support player for the far post, giving the ball dribbler the option of shooting or passing.
- When passing the ball, play it into the space behind the defensive line, for a teammate to run to.
- When making a run for a teammate, run for the open space, not into a crowded area.
- Draw defenders wide by making runs or dribbling the ball in that direction. When dribbling wide of the goal, take the ball all the way to the end line and then to the near post if possible. When the defenders move wide, cross the ball or cut it back diagonally to the middle for a teammate to shoot.
- Shoot the ball when within range of the goal.
- As a target player, post yourself about 12–14 yards out from the middle of the goal and lay a one-touch pass back to a teammate to shoot the ball.

Forwards, on defense in the attacking third

- If possession is lost, everyone runs back to mark an opponent and defend or to pressure defenders in possession of the ball, *including forwards!*

Playing without Pressure

Fullbacks, on offense in the defensive third

- Draw the opposing forwards to create space for teammates in the middle third.
- Make lateral passes to spread the opposing forwards wide.
- Play the ball to open space for teammates in the attacking third if there is space beyond the defense.
- When opposing forwards are spread out wide, dribble the ball between them.
- Make through passes to players who are dropping back ("checking back").
- Initiate the attack by making overlapping runs into the attacking third.
- As the ball moves upfield, keep pushing forward so that there is no gap between the midfield and the defensive third.

Midfielders, on offense in the middle third

- Check back to give your defender with the ball the chance for an outlet pass.
- When receiving the ball with your back turned, always look to pass it back to a supporting player who can see the entire field of play. Do not turn with the ball unless there is ample space.
- Play the ball to the space behind the defense for the forwards in the attacking third.
- If forwards are not in position to receive the ball, either hold it until they are or pass it laterally or behind to keep it moving and buy time.
- If there is space in the middle third, dribble the ball and penetrate into the attacking third until a defender commits to marking you, leaving one of your teammates open for a pass.

Forwards, on offense in the attacking third

- If possible, dribble the ball to the goal line and cut to the near post. This forces defenders to commit to you, freeing up teammates for a shot on goal.
- When crossing the ball, chip it to the far post or cut it back to the near post. This is most effective because as the defense sets up for the cross, it usually lines up parallel to the goal line. A low cross that follows this same line will most likely be cleared out by the defense. However, if the ball is cut back diagonally from the near post, it is very easy to pass the ball through a gap in the defensive line. Likewise, a ball chipped over the defenders will have a good chance of finding a teammate's head.
- When in range and when there are players obstructing the goalie's view of the ball, *shoot.*
- Do not hold the ball long, thus losing the opportunity for effective penetration.
- Gain as much ground as possible. Take as much space as the defense will give, forcing them to commit to the ball carrier. Once they are drawn out, look to play the ball to any space so a running teammate can either shoot, cross, or play the ball back for someone else to shoot.
- Always look to set others up for a cross or shot.

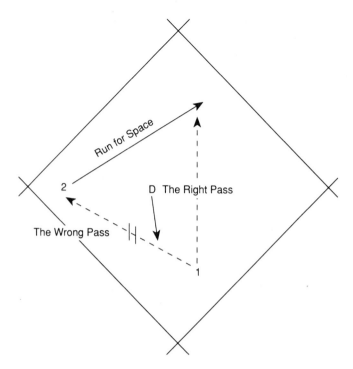

Figure 9.2
Making the outside pass.

Drills

The following drills should be of immense help for beginning players.

1. Check back, meet the ball, pass back, turn wide, and receive the ball again.
2. Two against one (2 v 1) in a 15-yard square. The intent is to make the outside pass. (See Figure 9.2.)
3. 3 v 2 keep-away. The ball carrier moves the least while the other two move constantly. After touching the ball, the defender switches positions with the player who touched it last. Restrict the playing space when players become more proficient.
4. 3 v 3 possession game with a free fourth player. The fourth plays on whichever team has the ball. Players alternate as the fourth.
5. 3 v 3 with small goals. The team in possession always has a player with the ball, one to assist, and a backup. The assisting player plays wide of the dribbler, making himself available for a pass. When one player passes to another, the roles change depending on the players' positions and who has the ball.
6. 4 v 4 teams (same as the last 3 v 3). The team in possession always has a player with the ball, one to assist, one to support, and a backup. These four roles change constantly as the ball is moved around. The support player works like another assist or backup player, as the situation demands.

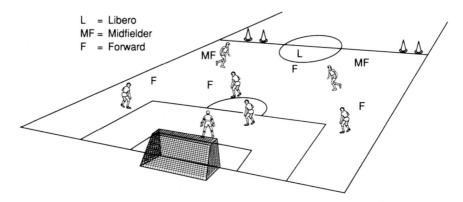

Figure 9.3
A game of 7 v 7 with three goals. The defenders are in silhouette.

7. 7 v 7 with three goals—one regular goal and two six-foot-wide goals, one on each side of the midfield line close to the touchline. Separate the teams so that the forwards and midfielders are defending the two small goals and the defenders are defending the normal-size goal.

In this drill, the forwards and three midfielders attempt to attack, shoot, score, and defend when possession is lost. They also learn to defend on both sides, since they have no backs behind them. (See Figure 9.3.) The defenders learn to stop the attack and attempt overlaps, attempting to score on either goal by switching the game from side to side as the forwards drop back and crowd one goal. The modern defender must know when to move up and start the attack and change the game in the middle, as well as keep possession.

Principles of Defense

10

All players have assigned defensive duties. A team defends as necessity dictates, whether as individuals, in small groups of two or three players, as a large group, or as a team of eleven.

Individual Defense

The easiest and best way to defend as an individual is to get to the ball before your opponent does. If under pressure clear the ball, kick far, high, and wide. It does not matter who should be covering whom or what someone's assignment is; if you can get to the ball, do so.

If your opponent gets to the ball before you, force him or her to lose control, partially or totally, by kicking it away. Alternatively, throw the attacker off balance—without committing a foul—with a nudge or other *legal* body contact. Some contact is part of the game, so use it to your advantage.

If an attacking player receives the ball with his or her back turned, do not allow him or her to turn upfield with it. Force the attacker to pass the ball back. An opponent facing your goal is far more dangerous than one who is not.

When an attacker approaches the area you are defending, run toward him or her as fast as possible. At the least, this slows the attacker down and keeps him or her farther from the goal. Once within ten feet, be sure that you have good balance. While slowing down, be ready to back up toward either side or straight back, or to tackle the ball if close enough. The attacker will often react to this initial charge by moving to beat the defender. Therefore, you must be ready to counter and take the ball away. If you decide not to counter, back up as slowly as necessary to maintain jockeying distance from the advancing attacker and thus gain time for your teammates to find their proper places or get ready to assist.

By partially challenging a ball carrier, the defender forces the attacker to take the path of least resistance, which should be the direction desired by the defender and the signal for the backup to tackle!

Two-Player Defense

In Figure 10.1, player A is attacking against B. Player C is in the attack; player D is defending with player B.

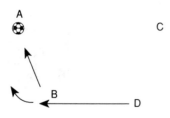

Figure 10.1

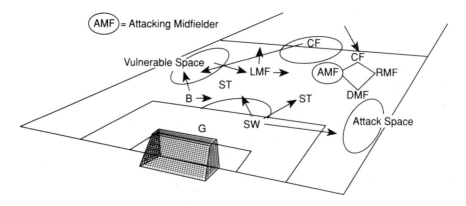

Figure 10.2
One-side-of-the-field defense. Arrows indicate areas players are expected to cover. Note the diamond defense stance.

Player A is moving forward with the ball. Player B fronts—that is, faces up to—A, partially forcing A to the outside (away from the goal) in a predictable direction. Player D leaves C to double-team A. As D goes by B, B follows about two steps back. Player A has no place to go forward and is intercepted by D and B. Player C will be marked by another midfielder.

Large-Group Defense

One-side-of-the-field defense. If the attackers lose the ball in the middle or last third, the midfield players come together in a diamond formation to stop the counterattack. One forward comes back to pressure; the other backs up to cover the area away from the play alongside the midfielders' diamond formation (see Figure 10.2). This diamond formation shifts as necessary over the entire width of the field. The defense recovers by forcing the offense to make long passes that, since they have been forced, are expected and can be intercepted. The opposition has a minimal chance of successfully penetrating the defense.

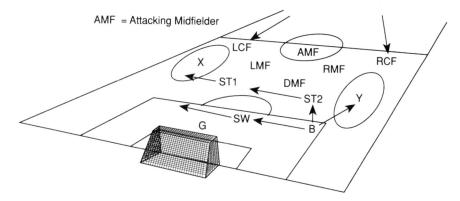

AMF = Attacking Midfielder

Figure 10.3
The role of the back (B) is very important: first, to cover space Y if the attack is directed there and RCF cannot recover; second, to have ST1 and ST2 slide over so ST1 can cover space X while B takes the place of ST2 or SW goes to X and B plays sweeper.

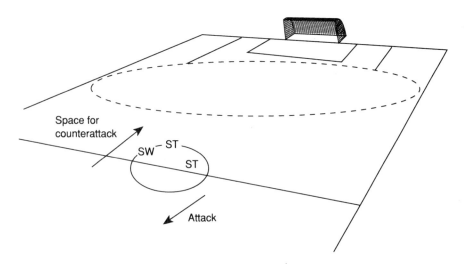

Figure 10.4
Note the space left by the attacking team behind their defense. This can be exploited by a structured plan of counterattack.

An advantage of this defense is that it does not give up too much territory, since the immediate defense—the players in front of the goalie—is complete. It is up to the midfielders and forwards to pressure the opposition on either side of the field. Less space means greater need for passing accuracy, less time for execution, less time to locate an open teammate, and therefore more chance to steal the ball and regain possession. (See Figure 10.3.) Further, this leaves the opposition with few players to defend their defensive half, leaving a vast space for a fast counterattack. (See Figure 10.4.)

To recapitulate, on the defense, players need to:

1. *Delay* until other teammates can respond.
2. *Withdraw,* buying time when they cannot hold their ground and stop an attacker.
3. *Force the direction* of the attack inside or outside, depending upon a predetermined plan.
4. *Approach and tackle.* This is the job of the backup player, who should be supporting whichever teammate is delaying the attacker.

When defending, a team should always have one target player to pass to, to signal the beginning of a prearranged counterattack.

Systems of Play

11

The beauty of soccer rests largely in its spontaneity and the freedom of action it allows its players. Individual initiative and spontaneity are essential to quality games. The wide range of self-expression possible also demands that players understand each others' limitations. Team members must work together to prevent failure.

The better their understanding of the game, the better participants' ability to respond correctly to immediate challenges. To facilitate better cooperation and increase teamwork, responsibilities must be divided and then developed among players. Within this framework, the players will take liberties, which will bring out each member's real potential and qualities. But if structure takes precedence, thus limiting the players' responsibilities, individual initiative and creative spontaneity will be stunted, even eliminated.

So whatever structure is proposed should allow for *personal interpretation* and *initiative*. Undoubtedly this philosophy will cause a few setbacks—to put it bluntly, losing some games. This is where the coach comes in. A capable coach should know how to encourage each player's individual qualities and then blend them all into an effective team.

The oldest system, used in the early 1900s, was the 2–3–5 system, meaning two fullbacks, three halfbacks, and five forwards. Of these five forwards, the center forward often fell back to the middle of the field, combined with the center halfback, made long passes to the wings, and moved up to score. (See Figure 11.1.)

In the 1920s, prompted by a change in the offside law, Herbert Chapman, the Arsenal club coach, started a new system in England. It was the WM system, or the 3–2–2–3, with three fullbacks, two halfbacks, two inside forwards, and three forwards. (As seen in Figure 11.2, the positioning of the players resembled the letters M and W when seen from the perspective of the defending goalie.) The new offside law required that there be at least two defenders between the attacking player and the goal line at the moment the ball is kicked by the attacking team.

The WM system persisted until the early 1960s, when the 4–2–4 was started in Brazil (see Figure 11.3). Then other formations emerged, such as the 4–3–3 (Figure 11.4), the 4–4–2 (Figure 11.5), the 5–3–2 (Figure 11.6), and the Catenaccio. Other formations developed from their variations. Presently the 4–4–2, when used against a team with the same system becomes a 3–5–2, 3 backs, 5 midfielders and 2 forwards.

The WM was basically a man-to-man system, while the 2–3–5 it replaced was a zone system. The WM persisted about 40 years and popularized the idea of man-to-man coverage, simplifying the players' duties.

The zone idea has persisted, however, and I continue to recommend it as the most complete way of bringing out *initiative, creativity,* and *spontaneity* in players. It is stimulating, challenging, and entertaining for both players and spectators. A player who is taught to play a zone style has much more complete knowledge of the game and a more versatile approach to all game situations. Of course, the athlete familiar with a zone style can play man to man if necessary.

Systems help organize teams and assign suitable tasks to personnel. However, once the game begins, no system can cover all variables; individual initiative, creativity, and intuition must take over. Systems will come and go, so coaches must regard them as limited measures to encourage understanding of the game and individual growth. This is why the player must first know the fundamentals of position play and the responsibilities that generally accompany particular positions. Remember, soccer is not a coach's game.

L/RW = Left/Right Wing
IL/IR = Inside Left/Right Forward
CF = Center Forward
L/RH = Left/Right Halfback
G = Goalie
L/RFB = Left/Right Fullback
CH = Center Halfback

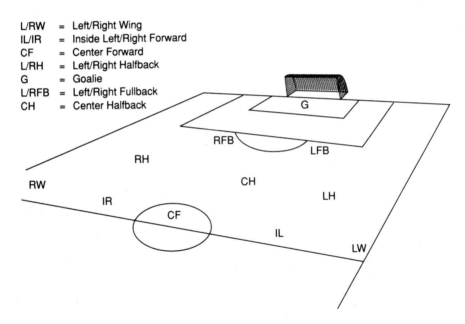

Figure 11.1
The 2–3–5 system—the oldest system in the game.

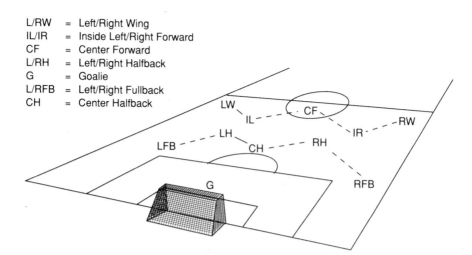

L/RW	= Left/Right Wing
IL/IR	= Inside Left/Right Forward
CF	= Center Forward
L/RH	= Left/Right Halfback
G	= Goalie
L/RFB	= Left/Right Fullback
CH	= Center Halfback

Figure 11.2
The WM system (3–2–2–3 system)—or MW as seen from the goalie's perspective.

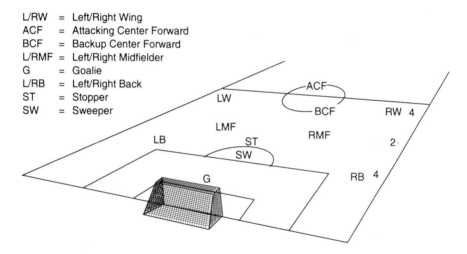

L/RW	= Left/Right Wing
ACF	= Attacking Center Forward
BCF	= Backup Center Forward
L/RMF	= Left/Right Midfielder
G	= Goalie
L/RB	= Left/Right Back
ST	= Stopper
SW	= Sweeper

Figure 11.3
The 4–2–4 system.

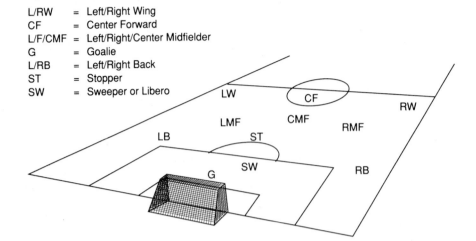

L/RW	= Left/Right Wing
CF	= Center Forward
L/F/CMF	= Left/Right/Center Midfielder
G	= Goalie
L/RB	= Left/Right Back
ST	= Stopper
SW	= Sweeper or Libero

Figure 11.4
The 4–3–3 system.

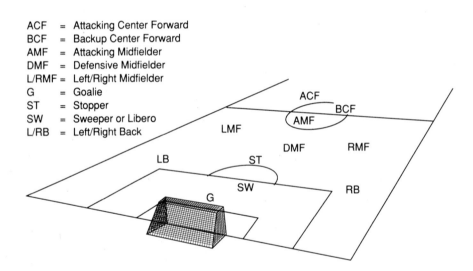

ACF	= Attacking Center Forward
BCF	= Backup Center Forward
AMF	= Attacking Midfielder
DMF	= Defensive Midfielder
L/RMF	= Left/Right Midfielder
G	= Goalie
ST	= Stopper
SW	= Sweeper or Libero
L/RB	= Left/Right Back

Figure 11.5
The 4–4–2 system.

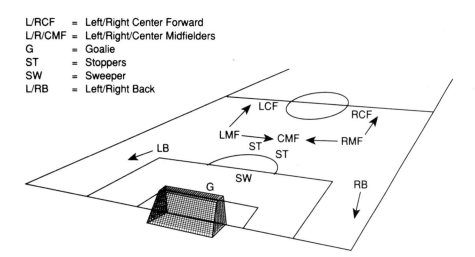

L/RCF   = Left/Right Center Forward
L/R/CMF = Left/Right/Center Midfielders
G   = Goalie
ST   = Stoppers
SW   = Sweeper
L/RB   = Left/Right Back

Figure 11.6
The 5–3–2 system. With LB and RB possibly moving up. Notice two wing fullbacks and two stoppers.

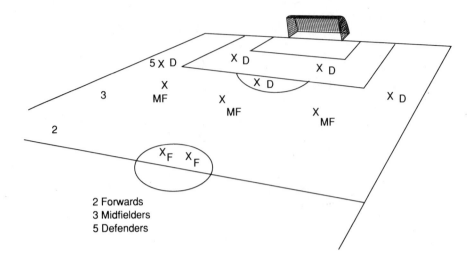

2 Forwards
3 Midfielders
5 Defenders

Catenaccio 1, notice one stopper dropping back at the sweeper level. Originally when Helenio Herrera used it, he had talented players able to attack from the back, thus, it was an attacking system. Copiers, not having adequate talent, eventually made it into a defensive system.

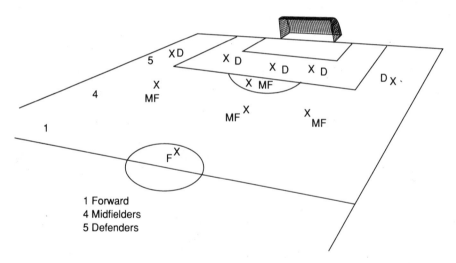

1 Forward
4 Midfielders
5 Defenders

Catenaccio 2, defensively it becomes a 5-1-3-1 formation with 9 players in the defensive third.

Glossary

The arc (p. 6)
An arc centered on the 18-yard line of the penalty area, with the center on the penalty spot and a 10-yard radius.

Aerobic (p. 40)
Endurance running using current oxygen intake.

Backs (pp. 49, 55)
Players in front of the goal with mainly defensive duties.

Backup (pp. 70, 73)
An assisting or supporting player for the player possessing the ball.

Backup center forward (pp. 49, 60)
An assisting center forward (when two forwards are used).

The ball (p. 7)
A sphere full of air, approved by FIFA. The number of panels, materials, size and pressure varies with ages of participants.

Bibs (p. 34)
Upper body contrasting colored panels or sleeveless loose T-shirts.

Blindside (p. 83)
The goalside area behind an opposing player.

Block (p. 98)
When a whole team moves together in attack or defense.

Body contact (correct) (p. 28)
Shoulder to shoulder.

Center forward (p. 60)
Usually the farthest player up in attack and goal scorer.

Channeling (pp. 70, 79)
Like jockeying—make an opponent advance with the ball in a predetermined course.

Checking or checking back (p. 100)
Coming back to receive a pass or draw an opponent to make space.

Chip (pp. 25, 76)
A short high pass over defenders.

Circuit training (p. 35)
A course with a number of stations incorporating various techniques related to soccer.

Clears   (p. 111)
Kicking the ball away from the danger area.

Corner flag   (p. 7)
A 5-foot *rigid* but nondangerous thin pole with a small flag at the top. Must not be moved when executing corner kicks. Placed where the touchline and goal line meet.

Corner kick area   (p. 6)
A 3-foot radius area connecting the side or touchline and the goal line with the center at the intersection of the goal and touchlines.

Cover   (p. 68)
Mark, play close to an opponent, to prevent him from receiving the ball.

Crossbar   (p. 5)
The bar connecting the two uprights, 8 foot from the ground.

Cross pass   (p. 25)
Mostly a high ball passed from players wide of the goal.

Defensive team   (p. 77)
The team not in possession of the ball.

Diamond defense   (p. 112)
A defensive pattern made by players in adjacent positions, crowding the path of attack.

Direct kick   (p. 13)
Awarded for a foul outside the penalty area. A goal can be scored from a direct kick.

Drill   (p. 38)
A repetitive technical or skillful exercise to promote intuitive responses in real game situations.

Drop kicking   (p. 54)
Used by goalies for a faster forward punt. The ball is struck the moment it rebounds from being dropped to the ground.

Dummy   (pp. 68, 69, Figure 6.3B)
When an intended receiver lets the pass go to another teammate, while faking and drawing a defender.

Fake   (pp. 65, 67)
A deceptive move intended to gain space and time.

Far post   (p. 5)
The upright farthest from the ball.

Forcing a foul   (p. 12)
An attacking player forces a defending opponent into making a foul when attempting to slow his/her progress or regain possession.

Forcing the play   (pp. 70, 79)
Guiding the attacker to a predetermined area.

Free player   (p. 79)
A player unmarked by an opponent.

Goal kick (p. 15)
Taken by defensive team to restart the game, after the ball last touched by the attacking team passed the goal line, but not inside the goal.

Goal posts (p. 5)
The two upright posts holding the crossbar and framing the goal.

Goalie (p. 76)
Protects the goal and can use his or her hands in the penalty area.

Goalkeeper area (p. 6)
A 20-yard × 6-yard area starting on the goal line, inside the penalty area, where the goalie should not be challenged.

Goalside (p. 68)
The path between a forward and the defensive goal or near post, best occupied by defensive players.

Grid (p. 37)
A number of equal-size squares in each of which a limited number of players can participate.

Halfbacks (p. 49)
Play immediately in front of the fullbacks from touchline to touchline.

Indirect kick (p. 13)
A second player must touch the ball in order for a goal to be awarded.

Instep kick (p. 23)
Kicking the ball with the shoelace area of the foot.

Jockey/Jockeying (pp. 70, 79)
Delaying, slowing down an opponent in possession of the ball with the intent of winning the ball.

Kick off (p. 10)
The ball kicked by the offensive team at the start, halftime or after a goal is scored. The ball must travel forward of the center line the distance of its circumference before it can be played by another player.

Libero (p. 57)
An attacking sweeper occasionally moving up from the back.

Marking (p. 68)
Playing close to an opponent to prevent or hinder him/her in receiving the ball.

Medicine ball (p. 35)
A heavy 6–12-pound ball used for conditioning and the overload principle.

Midfielders (p. 49)
Link players between backs and forwards.

Morphology (p. 34)
Inherited or developed physical characteristics.

Near post (p. 5)
The upright closest to the ball.

Negative player (pp. 97, 100)
A player from the defensive team, left behind the ball.

Offensive team   (p. 100)
The team in possession of the ball.

Overlapping   (p. 87)
When a back advances up field over the positions of midfielders or forwards.

Penalty area   (p. 6)
A rectangular area in front of the goal 44 × 18 yards where only the goalie can use his/her hands. For any foul or hand ball in this area by the defending team, a penalty will be awarded to be taken from the "penalty spot."

Penalty box   (p. 6)
Same as penalty area.

Penalty spot   (p. 6)
A spot 9 inches in diameter, 12 yards away from the center of the defending goal.

The pendulum   (p. 30, 35)
A ball hanging from a cord.

Peripheral vision   (pp. 21, 45)
Lateral and vertical vision, while focusing in a center area. Indirect vision.

Place (to place)   (p. 26)
To make an accurate pass or shot to a small area.

Pressure   (pp. 102, 107)
Close marking.

Read   (p. 45)
To anticipate one's intentions.

Red card   (p. 13)
Ejection from the game.

Restart   (p. 31)
A dead ball situation, when the referee stops the game.

Rhythm   (pp. 41, 96)
The intensity or tempo of the game.

Set pieces   (p. 31)
A set play, executed only in selected situations.

Shielding   (p. 66)
The ability to control the ball in order to gain time.

Short pass   (p. 26)
A pass intended to draw the receiver to meet the ball.

Show   (p. 103)
To come back and make yourself available for a pass.

Skill   (p. 17)
Technique under pressure.

Slide tackle   (pp. 28, 29)
Sliding into the ball to dispossess an opponent.

Space (pp. 84, 85)
An area to pass the ball or to receive it in order to delay or prevent defensive coverage.

Stopper (p. 56)
Tight marking backs.

Stripped (p. 106)
Lost the ball.

Sweepers (pp. 56, 57)
Free support men for stoppers and backs.

Tackle (p. 28)
Stopping the progress of an offensive player by blocking the ball while in his possession.

Tactics (pp. 65, 77)
A style of play forcing the opponent in a predictable, unavoidable stance, that can be exploited.

Takeover (p. 87)
Shielding and allowing an incoming teammate to take one's ball, confusing defenders.

Target player (pp. 60, 70)
A player, an intended receiver, able to control, delay and distribute the ball.

Through ball (p. 86, fig. 7.10)
A forward pass to the space behind a defender.

Touchline (p. 6)
The side lines of the soccer field playing area.

Traffic (p. 97)
Too many crowded players.

The tunnel (p. 35)
An enclosed area 20 yard–30 yard long, used for precision power shooting.

Turning (p. 72)
A player receiving the ball facing his own goal.

Vision (p. 45)
The ability to anticipate a positive situation.

Wall pass (p. 84)
A diagonal pass—to be sent right back, at a 90-degree angle to the running original passer.

Weak-side (p. 105)
The side with the least number of defensive players.

Wing backs (outside backs) (pp. 49, 55)
Backs playing wide close to the touchline.

Yellow card (p. 13)
Warning for serious infraction.

Zone (p. 116)
Playing by covering a certain area rather than an opposing player.

Index